THE CHURCH OF THE NEW TESTAMENT: ITS ORGANIZATION AND FUNCTIONS

A SEMI-PROGRAMMED TEXTBOOK

Sam Westman Burton

Wipf and Stock Publishers
EUGENE, OREGON

Wipf and Stock Publishers
199 West 8th Avenue, Suite 3
Eugene, Oregon 97401

The Church of the New Testament: Its Organization and Functions
A Semi-Programmed Textbook
By Burton, Sam Westman
Copyright©2001 Burton, Sam Westman
ISBN: 1-57910-833-4
Publication date: December, 2001
Previously published by NPP, 2001.

FOREWORD

The author, Sam W. Burton, has seen a need for trained leadership in churches, young and old. This volume is his answer to that need, drawn from his experience and that of many others. I would have been glad to have had this study manual for sessions of elders in churches I have pastored as well as for leaders in house churches that I have helped plant overseas.

This study has been field-tested and found useful and adaptable. Its value is enhanced by its non-threatening simplicity. Those using it soon find, "I can do it." Or find, "Help is close at hand, and I can correct my mistakes right away." For the poorly educated this is a God-send, giving hope and satisfaction. For the illiterate the statements with blanks can be formulated as questions for them to answer.

This study has already been used in other languages, and may God extend its use more widely among the nations of His world. In homes and storefronts, tents and under shade trees, tenements and caves - wherever the church is gathered - may these pages bring understanding and joy, worship and holy ministry.

David Brainerd Woodward

INTRODUCTION

There are many good studies about the doctrine of the church (ecclesiology). We don't pretend to repeat the teachings of these books. But there is still confusion about the Biblical organization and functions of the local church. In this text we are going to study some aspects of the local church or a group of believers met together.

The word "Ecclesia" in the New Testament can be translated with the words, "church, assembly, or congregation." When we use the word "church," many times we think of a building or a temple. We say, "Let's go to church." But the word means an organism and not something material. We will use the word in this sense of organism or believers met in His Name. The local church, of course, is part of the universal church. This study can be used as a supplement or is also complete in itself.

The study reflects the teachings of the book <u>New Testament Order For Church and Missionary</u> by Alexander R. Hay. My experiences on the mission field for 22 years in church planting in Uruguay and the Amazon River in Brazil, and 14 years in Theological Education by Extension in Mexico also contributed to the elaboration of the theme.

Acknowledgements

Betsy Burton, my lifelong wife and missionary companion, has worked very hard to back translate this study from Portuguese to English. Thank you, Betsy! We also want to thank Carrie Mann and Heather Bright, students from Christian Heritage College, who worked hard putting this manuscript on the computer.

In this study, we consider the position of the plurality of elders in the local church and the Lord's Table as a worship meeting. This study is also available in Spanish and Portuguese.

We trust that this study will be a blessing in the church and for the glory of the Lord Jesus Christ.

Sam W. Burton

INSTRUCTIONS

1. Complete the first item, writing the correct word in the blank space.

2. Is it correct? To be sure, look at the next paragraph at the beginning of the next item, number 2.

3. In the same way, the answer to item 2 is found in the beginning of item 3. The answer, then, is found in the parenthesis of the following item.

4. Another way to answer the items in this book is to mark or check the correct answer.

5. The two ways used to answer the items in this study are to write or mark the correct answer.

6. You should always answer the item first and afterward look at or confirm the correct answer. You may want to use a card to cover the confirmation until you've written your answer.

7. Remember the method: **READ, WRITE** or **MARK** and then **CONFIRM** the correct answer.

8. The Bible translation used in this study is from the NKJV (New King James Version).

CONTENTS

<u>LESSON</u>   <u>PAGE</u>

1. The Teaching of Jesus Christ--The Universal Church 4

2. The Teaching of Jesus Christ--The Local Church 9

3. The New Testament Church Began on the Day of Pentecost 14

4. Jerusalem--The First Local Church 21

5. The Fellowship of the Local Church 28

6. The Lord's Table 36

7. The Lord's Table (Supper): Warning and Frequency of Celebration . . 45

8. The Prayer Meeting 55

9. The Body of Christ: The Manifestations of the Holy Spirit 67

10. The Offices or Positions in the Local Church: Elders (Presbyters,

    Bishops, Pastors) and Deacons 80

11. Discipline or Separation in the Local Church 90

12. The Principal Mission of the New Testament Church 102

Appendixes 109

    Exams for the Study

    Chart of the Gifts

    Bibliography

LESSON 1   THE TEACHING OF JESUS CHRIST,
THE UNIVERSAL CHURCH

Upon finishing this lesson, the student will be able to:

--Understand to whom the church belongs?

--Explain what the Universal Church is.

--State the promise of Jesus Christ with regard to the victorious church.

1. Read the words of the Lord Jesus in Matthew 16:18, "I will build My church, and the gates of Hades shall not prevail against it." The person speaking in this passage is _____ _____.

2. (Jesus Christ) This passage teaches us that the church belongs to _____ _____.

3. (Jesus Christ) The word that expresses this truth is the word _____.

4. (My) According to the verse, the builder of the church is _____.

5. (Jesus or Christ) When Jesus pronounced these words, the church . . . (Mark the correct answer)

A. _____ existed in the past.

B. _____ existed at the time of the words.

C. _____ is still in the future.

6. (C) The first promise of the Lord Jesus is "_____ _____ _____ _____ _____."

7. (I will build my church) In this passage the church did not yet exist. Jesus is speaking about the universal church and not the _____ church.

8. (local) Jesus was speaking about the _____ church.

9. (Universal) We should now consider the significance of the words "Universal Church." The words do not signify a building, or a denomination, or a congregation of local believers. It refers to the large company of individual believers from the Day of Pentecost who have believed in the Lord Jesus Christ as their Lord and Savior. It is an eternal and universal, visible and invisible company joined to Christ by faith, ". . . He chose us in Him before the foundation of the world . . ." (Eph. 1:4). The Universal Church does not mean a _____ or a _____ or a _____ of local believers.

10. (building, denomination, congregation) The Universal Church is composed of all the believers in Christ since Pentecost. All these believers belong to the _____ _____.

11. (Universal Church) Read again Matthew 16:18 noticing especially the last phrase. In this phrase we notice the second promise of the Lord Jesus in regard to the church: ". . . the _____ of _____ _____ _____ _____ against her," the Universal Church.

12. (gates, Hades, shall not prevail) The words, "The gates of hell (or Hades)" refer to the power or dominion and the person of Satan and the hosts of evil. But _____ cannot conquer the church that belongs to Christ.

13. (Satan) Many times it seems that Satan, the enemy of the church, is conquering a local church, but it is a comfort to know that finally, ". . . the _____ of _____ cannot _____ against it," the Universal Church.

14. (gates, Hades, prevail) When Jesus said, "I will build my church," He was speaking of the _____ _____.

15. (Universal Church) The church belongs to _____ _____.

16. (Jesus Christ) Jesus promised, "_____ _____ _____ my church."

17. (I will build) Jesus also promised that His church is a conquering or victorious church. The church of Christ is a _____ or _____ _____.

18. (conquering, victorious church).

Suggestions and Plan for the Group Study:

Lesson 1: The Teaching of Jesus Christ concerning the Universal Church

Plan:

1. See that the students have already studied the lesson. (Done their homework!)

2. Read Biblical passages related to the theme of the lesson.

3. Use the following questions or references to stimulate discussion and exchange of ideas.

Questions and References:

1. What is the context of Matthew 16:18? Read Matthew 16:13-20.

2. What do the words, ". . . upon this rock" mean? What rock?

3. Discuss the words, ". . . the gates of Hades shall not prevail against it?" Is this true?

4. Note the definition of the Universal Church in Ephesians 1:22,23.

LESSON 2 THE TEACHING OF JESUS CHRIST

THE LOCAL CHURCH

Upon finishing this lesson, the student will be able to:

- Define the local church

- State the promise of the Lord Jesus with regard to believers met together.

- Explain the context of the verses mentioned.

19. We will now study another passage or teaching of the Lord Jesus about the church. Read Matthew 18:15-20. The theme of this portion is, "Dealing with a sinning brother" or "Discipline in the future church." We will not deal with this now. We want to notice verse 17 of this passage. In this verse we notice the word _____ twice.

20. (church) Now it is impossible to bring a case of discipline before the Universal Church because it is dispersed throughout the world. For this reason the church mentioned in this passage is the _____ _____.

21. (local church) The local church is that part of the universal church which meets together in a place or locality. The local church is a part of the

_____ _____.

22. (Universal Church) In Matthew 16:18, Jesus was speaking about, (mark the correct answer).

   A. _____ a denomination

   B. _____ a local church

   C. _____ the Universal Church

23. (C) Did you get it right? Jesus was speaking about the Universal Church, but in Matthew 18:17, Jesus was speaking about the _____ _____.

24. (local church) The local church is a group of believers "chosen by God" who meet in some _____.

25. (locality or place) Now let's study Matthew, chapter 18, verse 20. The theme is still the matter of a sinning brother but in verse 18 it talks about "binding" and "loosing," and in verse 19 about prayer. Verse 20 then is talking about the local church is prayer. Verse 20 speaks about the _____ _____ in prayer.

26. (local church) Here, perhaps, we have a definition of the local church in

its simplicity, ". . . two or three are gathered together in my name." The name here is the name of _____.

27. (Jesus or Christ) The local church can be very simple, only "two or three." One person alone cannot be considered a church or assembly or a congregation. One person alone cannot be a _____ _____.

28. (local church) The two or three are met together as a church in fellowship with Christ and not only as individuals. A very simple definition of a local church is "_____ or _____ are _____ _____ in _____ _____."

29. (two, three, gathered together, my name) A blessed promise of the Lord Jesus to believers truly met in His name is, "I am there in the midst of them." ("There am I with them.") Jesus promised His _____ with the local church met in His name.

30. (presence) The local church can be very simple but it must be met in His _____.

31. (Name) This name is the name of _____.

32. (Jesus or Christ) A local church has a precious promise: the _____ of _____.

33. (presence, Jesus or Christ) In Matthew 18:17, Jesus spoke of the _____ _____.

34. (local church) A local church is composed of true believers met together in the name of _____.

35. (Jesus or Christ) The simplest local church would be _____ or _____ believers.

36. (two, three) A most precious promise for the church met together in the _____ of _____ _____.

37. (presence, Jesus Christ)

Suggestions and Plan for the Study Group:

Lesson 2: The Teaching of the Lord Jesus concerning the Local Church

Plan:

1. Check to see that the students have already studied the lesson or reserve time for the study.

2. Read Bible passages related to the theme.

3. Use the following questions to motivate an exchange of ideas.

Questions and References:

1. What is the theme of the context of Matthew 18:15-20?

2. What is a local church?

3. What is the difference between a local church and the Universal Church?

4. What is the simplest local church?

5. What is the promise of the Lord Jesus to true Christians met together in His Name. What does this mean to you?

LESSON 3   THE NEW TESTAMENT CHURCH BEGAN
ON THE DAY OF PENTECOST

Upon finishing this lesson, the student will be able to:

-- Consider the promises of Jesus regarding the coming of the Comforter or Helper (Paraclete).

-- Know when the New Testament church began.

-- Understand the importance of I Corinthians 10:32.

40. We have already seen in the first lesson that the church was still future when Jesus spoke the words in Matthew 16:18. When Jesus spoke the words in Matthew 16:18, the church was still in the _____.

41. (future) If this is true, when then did the church begin? Let's remember that the church, "the Body of Christ," was a "mystery hidden in God." (Read Ephesians 3:3-6). It was something not precisely revealed in the Old Testament. The church was a _____ hidden in God.

42. (mystery) Let's notice some words of the Lord Jesus before His death, resurrection and ascension. Read John 14:16,17, 20, and 26: "And I will pray to the Father, and he shall give you another Comforter . . . the Spirit of Truth . . . ye know him; for he dwelleth with you, and shall be in you

". . . at that day ye shall know that I am in my Father and ye in me, and I in you . . . But the Comforter, which is the Holy Spirit, whom the Father will send in my name . . . ."

In these verses Jesus promised to His disciples another _____.

43. (Comforter) In these verses (please read them again) There are two other names given to the Comforter. They are: _____ of _____ and _____ _____.

44. (Spirit, Truth, and Holy Spirit) The one who would send the Comforter, the Holy Spirit, is the _____.

45. (Father) These verses teach us also that the Holy Spirit was with them but was not yet in them. Did the Holy Spirit live in the hearts or the lives of the disciples?

A. _____ yes
B. _____ no

46. (B) The words "in that day" are words that express (in the context):

A. _____ the past
B. _____ the present
C. _____ the future

47. (C) Yes, they are words in the future. And there is a precious truth: When the Holy Spirit comes, there will be an intimate and precious union between the Father, the Son, and His own. It is expressed in the words: ". . . ye shall know that I am in _____ _____, and ye _____ _____, and I _____ _____."

48. (My Father, in me, in you) Good! Let's look at two more passages. Read Acts 1:5 and 8. The words, :". . . but ye shall be baptized with the Holy Spirit not many days hence. . . But ye shall receive power, after that the Holy Spirit is come upon you . . ." (the underlined words) are in _____ time.

49. (future) Now! When were these words and promises fulfilled? Read Acts 2:1-4. Did you read them? Good! In verse one it says, "And when the day of Pentecost was fully come, they (some 120 persons) were all with one accord in one place." The Holy Spirit came in verse 4, "And they were all filled with the Holy Spirit." All the past words and promises were fulfilled on the Day of _____.

50. (Pentecost) The Holy Spirit came on the Day of _____.

51. (Pentecost) When did the Church begin? The church began on the Day of _____.

52. (Pentecost) When did the Comforter come? When did the disciples become intimately one with the Father and the Son? When were the disciples baptized with (or in) the Holy Spirit? On the _____ of _____.

53. (Day, Pentecost) Read I Corinthians 12:13, "For by one Spirit we were all baptized into one body--whether Jews or Greeks, whether slaves or free--and all have been made to drink into one Spirit." Since Pentecost every true believer, every person "chosen by God," is baptized by the Spirit into "the Body of Christ" where there is neither race nor social class. Every true believer, every true "child of God," is a member of the _____ of _____.

54. (Body of Christ, church of Christ) There is another very important passage for us to understand the program of God in this age of grace. Look at I Corinthians 10:32, "Give no offense, neither to the Jews or to the Greeks or to the church of God." The apostle Paul teaches us the divisions of humanity in this dispensation of the church. They are: the _____, the _____ and the _____ of

_____.

55. (Jews, Greeks, church, God) The Jews are the people of God of the Old Testament chosen from the days of Abraham. The Greeks (Gentiles) are those who are not Jews (or of the nations) of all epochs. And the church of God is composed of those who are converted from among the Jews and Greeks (Gentiles) since Pentecost. The church of God is composed of _____ and _____ since _____.

56. (Jews, Greeks, Pentecost) The church belongs to _____ _____.

57. (Jesus Christ) Jesus promised, "_____ _____ _____ my church."

58. (I will build) Jesus said that the simplest church consists where "_____ or _____ are gathered together in _____ _____."

59. (two, three, My name) The Helper or Comforter, the Holy Spirit, came on the Day of _____.

60. (Pentecost) The _____ began on the Day of Pentecost.

61. (church) The church of God consists of _____ and _____ converted to Christ.

62. (Jews, Greeks or Gentiles)

Suggestions and Plan for the Group Study:

Lesson 3: The New Testament Church Began on the Day of Pentecost

Plan:

1. Check to see that the students have already completed the lesson or reserve time for the study.

2. Read Bible passages related to the theme.

3. Use the following questions or references to motivate an exchange of ideas.

Questions and References:

1. When did the New Testament church begin?

2. Does the church of Christ exist in the Old Testament?

3. What is the relationship between the beginning of the church and the coming of the Holy Spirit?

4. When today is the believer baptized by the Holy Spirit?

5. In I Corinthians 10:32, what is the difference between the Jews, the Greeks, and the church of God?

LESSON 4   JERUSALEM, THE FIRST LOCAL CHURCH

Upon finishing this lesson, the student will be able to:

--Cite the location of the first local church.

--State the results of Peter's sermon.

--List the four activities of this church according to Acts 2:42.

--Explain the importance of Bible study in the local church.

63. We have already seen how the church began on the Day of Pentecost. On that day Peter preached his great discourse concerning the Lord Jesus Christ. Let's see now the results. Read Acts 2:41-47. Have you read the passage? What marvelous things happened that day! All these things happened in the city of Jerusalem. We can say that the first local church began in the city of _____.

64. (Jerusalem) The first _____ _____ began in Jerusalem.

65. (local church) We wish to notice some of the activities of this new congregation. Let's notice first of all the participants in these activities. In verse 41, we read, "then those who gladly received his word were baptized; and that day about three thousand souls were added to them." The people who received the word were _____.

66. (baptized) There were many people saved that day, about _____ _____ persons.

67. (three thousand) Before considering verse 42 in more detail, let's notice some of the things that happened in verses 43 to 47:

   43--everyone kept feeling a sense of awe (fear came upon every soul) and many wonders and signs were done
   44--". . . all who believed were together, and had all things in common."
   45--they showed their love in practical ways
   46--they continued with one accord in the temple, breaking bread from house to house, and ate their meals together
   47--they were praising God and having favor with all the people

   The result of this reverence for God, the unity of the believers, the love, the perseverance, the joy and praise were such that the Lord added to their number day by day. The result of walking with each other in love is the _____ of the church.

68. (growth) What joy! What blessing! Let's now consider verse 42 and the simple organization of the church in Jerusalem. The verse says: "And they continued steadfastly in the apostles' doctrine (teaching) and

fellowship (communion), in the breaking of bread, and in prayers."

The verse says that they continued or were faithful in four activities:

1. the teaching (doctrine) of the _____.

2. and _____

3. the _____ ___ _____

4. and _____

69. (apostles, fellowship, breaking of bread, prayers) Let's consider each activity in order. First, we notice that they continued diligently in the _____ _____.

70. (apostles' teaching or doctrine) The newly baptized believers began immediately to study the Bible. Without doubt they studied the Old Testament and the fulfilled prophecies concerning Jesus Christ, the promised Messiah. Without doubt they studied concerning the person of _____ _____.

71. (Jesus Christ) They studied all the words that Jesus had left with his disciples. Jesus promised in John 16:13 the following: "However when He, the Spirit of truth, has come, He will guide you into all truth; for He will not speak on His own authority, but whatever He hears He will

speak; and He will tell you things to come." We note that in the last two phrases the Holy Spirit would bring to their minds the words of Jesus and also disclose future things. One part of the apostle's teaching was the _____ of _____.

72. (words, Jesus) Another part concerned _____ things.

73. (future) At the time of Acts 4:42, the teaching of the apostles was still oral, that is, not yet written. But now we have the words of Jesus and the teaching or doctrine of the apostles in the New Testament. Because of this, we should study the Old Testament and the ___ _____.

74. (New Testament) The local church (a congregation together) needs to study the Bible or all the Word of God. This study can be in the Sunday School, a weekly Bible study, a spiritual retreat or in other gatherings. The important thing is that the local church have its _____ _____.

75. (Bible study) The word in Acts 2:42 "devoting" or "continued steadfastly" not only has the sense of studying but also the sense of obeying. The local church needs to _____ and _____ the teaching of the apostles or the _____.

76. (study, obey, Bible) The four activities of the Jerusalem were (see item 68):

   1. to study and obey the _____ of the _____.

   2. maintain _____.

   3. the _____ of _____.

   4. continue in _____.

77. (teaching, apostles, fellowship, breaking, bread, prayers) In our local congregations we need always to study the Bible or the _____ of _____.

78. (Word, God) One of the important activities of the church is to maintain its _____ _____.

79. (Bible study) The first activity of the church in Jerusalem was to continue in the _____ of the _____.

80. (teaching or doctrine, apostles) We call this activity _____ _____.

81. (Bible study) Each group of believers should have its _____ _____.

82. (Bible study)

Suggestions and Plan for the Group Study:

Lesson 4: Jerusalem, the First Local Church

Plan:

1. Be sure the students have already studied the lesson or reserve time for the study.

2. Read passages related to the subject.

3. Use the following questions or references to motivate the exchange of ideas.

Questions and References:

1. Where did the first local church begin?

2. What was the result of the preaching of Peter?

3. What did the believers study as a group?

4. In Acts 2:41-47, what were the activities of the church in those days?

5. What were the evidences of God's blessing upon the new church?

6. What is the importance of Bible study in your church?

7. What was the importance of baptism in the Christian church?

LESSON 5 THE FELLOWSHIP OF THE LOCAL CHURCH

Upon finishing this lesson, the student will be able to:

--State the significance of the word "fellowship."

--Explain the call of God to have fellowship with Jesus.

--Define God's purpose in our announcing the Gospel according to I John 1:3.

--Discuss the importance of Hebrews 10:25 in the life of the church.

83. We have already seen that the first activity of a local church is to have a Bible study. In Acts 2:42, the second thing mentioned is, ". . . and fellowship." The local church should have _____.

84. (fellowship) What does "fellowship" mean? The word in Greek is "KOINONIA" and can mean "communion," "sharing," "partnership," "participation," or "contribution." Also it refers to the Lord's Supper as in the expressions "sharing in (or communion of) the blood of Christ" and "sharing in (or communion of) the body of Christ" in I Corinthians 10:16. But in the context of the uses of the word, we would suggest that the fellowship means "meeting together," "intimacy," "being together in fellowship." The local church should have _____ together.

85. (fellowship) Let's study some verses that express these thoughts. In I Corinthians 1:9, we read, "God is faithful, by whom you were called into the fellowship of His Son, Jesus Christ our Lord." Paul teaches us that the believers in Corinth were called into the _____ of Jesus Christ.

86. (fellowship) How precious! We, as believers, are called to fellowship with Jesus Christ. We are called to have an intimate and eternal relationship with Jesus. The believer is called to have _____ with _____.

87. (fellowship, Jesus Christ) This fellowship with Jesus signifies participating in the life of Jesus, listening to and obeying His word and maintaining a time of prayer. The believer has the privilege of maintaining _____ with Jesus.

88. (fellowship) God calls the believer into the "_____ of His _____, _____ _____."

89. (fellowship, Son, Jesus Christ) See other verses such as II Corinthians 13:14, ". . . the fellowship (communion) of the Holy Spirit. . ." and Philippians 2:1, ". . . if fellowship of the Spirit." The believer can

experience the _____ of the _____ _____.

90. (fellowship, Holy Spirit) This fellowship with Christ and with the Spirit as individual believers in the basis of fellowship as believers together in Christ. We have already seen that the local church can be "where two or three are gathered together in My name . . . ." This name is the name of _____.

91. (Jesus) The two or three or more are _____ _____ in the name of Jesus.

92. (gathered together) In Galatians 2:9, the Apostle Paul wrote, ". . . perceived the grace that had been given to me, they gave me and Barnabus the <u>right hand of fellowship</u> . . . ." Without doubt there was an "agreement of ideas" and an acceptance of one another in love and ministry. Paul and Barnabus had _____ with the other apostles.

93. (fellowship) Another important passage is I John 1:3, ". . . that which we have seen and heard we declare to you, that you also may have <u>fellowship</u> with us; and truly our <u>fellowship</u> is with the Father and with His Son Jesus Christ." What a precious word! The Apostle John teaches us that

the purpose of proclaiming the gospel is to have brothers and sisters in the family. ". . . that you also may have <u>fellowship</u> with us." The desire of John and his colleagues in the faith is to maintain _____ among believers.

94. (fellowship) The purpose of preaching the gospel is that God's family may grow and have fellowship, oneness and togetherness among believers in Christ. A purpose among believers in Christ is to maintain _____ among themselves.

95. (fellowship) Please read I John 1:3 again. In the last phrase John writes "and truly our <u>fellowship</u> is with the Father, and with His Son Jesus Christ." We have already seen that the believer is called to the fellowship of Jesus and the fellowship of the Holy Spirit. Now we have fellowship with the Father. The true believer maintains fellowship with the _____, with the _____ and with the _____ _____.

96. (Father, Son, Holy Spirit) As individual believers and as believers together we should maintain fellowship with the _____, with the _____ and with the _____ _____.

97. (Father, Son, Holy Spirit) What is the practical meaning of these truths? How can we apply these truths in a local church? Read Hebrews 10:24, 25, ". . . and let us consider one another in order to stir up love and good works, not forsaking the assembling of ourselves together . . . ." Believers should stimulate ___ _____ to _____ and _____ _____.

98. (one another, love, good works) As believers we should maintain fellowship, consideration, love and good deeds (works). And we should not _____ our _____ together.

99. (forsake, assembling or meeting) Other translations say: "Not forsaking our congregation (or assembly)," "Not abandoning . . . the custom of attending the meetings," "Not giving up our duties in the church, neither the meetings." Without doubt there is much teaching in this sentence concerning the question of moving from one congregation to another, etc. But in this study we wish to stay with the question of one local church in fellowship. For the believers to maintain fellowship, they have to be together in the meetings. For the believers of one local church to maintain fellowship they have to attend the _____ of the church.

100. (meetings) The physical and spiritual presence of the believer in the meetings of the church is necessary to experience full fellowship with other believers. For a member of the church, his presence is necessary in the _____.

101. (meetings) The believer ought to have some active participation in all the meetings of the church to show his/her full _____.

102. (fellowship) When we think of the church in Jerusalem in "fellowship," we think of the believers together in all the activities of the congregation. Fellowship results from their love one for another. The believer in fellowship shows love in his desire to be _____.

103. (together) The local church should have _____ together.

104. (fellowship) The believer is called to have _____ with _____ Christ.

105. (fellowship, Jesus) Also the believer is able to experience fellowship of the _____ _____. (See item 89.)

106. (Holy Spirit) In I John 1:3, John teaches us that "our fellowship is with

the _____ and with His Son Jesus Christ."

107. (Father) Hebrews 10:25 tells us not to _____ our _____ _____.

108. (forsake, meeting together) To show one practical means of fellowship, the believer should be in the _____ of the _____.

109. (meetings, church or congregation)

Suggestions and Plan for the Group Study:

Lesson 5: The Fellowship of the Local Church

Plan:

1. Be sure the students have already studied the lesson or reserve time for the study.

2. Read passages related to the subject.

3. Use the following questions or references to motivate the exchange of ideas.

Questions and References:

1. What are the various definitions for the word "fellowship" and its application in the life of the church?

2. What is the significance of our fellowship with God and with believers in Christ? Study I John 1:3.

3. What is the importance of believers being in the meetings and activities of the congregation? See Hebrews 10:23-25.

LESSON 6   THE LORD'S TABLE

Upon finishing this lesson, the student will be able to:

--List the names used for the Lord's Table.

--Understand who instituted the Lord's Table and when.

--Tell to others the significance of this memorial feast.

--Give a short exposition of I Corinthians 11:23-26.

110. We have studied two activities of the first local church. The first local church was founded in the city of _____.

111. (Jerusalem) In that church we find them studying the Apostles' doctrine and maintaining fellowship together. A third activity mentioned in Acts 2:42 is "the _____ of _____."

112. (breaking, bread) What does "the breaking of bread" signify? We find the same phrase in Acts 20:7: "Now on the first day of the week, when the disciples came together to break bread." The majority of commentaries agree that this phrase refers to the Lord's Supper. The phrase "breaking of bread" refers to the _____.

113. (Lord's Supper or Table) Before considering some things in regard to the

Lord's Table, it will be good to notice the names used for this meeting or celebration. The name here in Acts 2:42 is "_____ of _____."

114. (breaking, bread) In the previous lesson we have already seen the phrases in I Corinthians 10:16, ". . . the communion of the blood of Christ?" ". . . the communion of the body of Christ." From these phrases the name that we use for the Lord's Supper is _____.

115. (communion) In I Corinthians 10:21, we find the words, ". . . partake of the Lord's table." The name here is _____.

116. (Lord's table) Following in I Corinthians, Paul deals with some abuses at the believers' meeting. In I Corinthians 11:20 he wrote, "therefore when you come together in one place, it is not to eat the Lord's supper." In this verse the name used is the _____.

117. (Lord's supper) Later on in the chapter, in verses 24 and 26, we read, "Do this in remembrance of me." (See also Luke 22:19.) The name here is "in _____ of ____."

118. (remembrance, me) The Catholic church uses the word "Eucharist." This

word in I Corinthians 14:16 comes from the Greek and is translated, "action of grace" (giving of thanks). When we are remembering the Lord Jesus in His death for us, we are offering an _____ of _____.

119. (action, grace) Now let us see if you are able to remember the names used for this meeting of the church. See the items 113 to 118. The names used are:

1. The _____ of _____, 113
2. _____, 114
3. The _____ _____, 115
4. The _____ _____, 116
5. In _____ of ____, 117
6. _____ or _____ of _____, 118

120. (1. breaking, bread; 2. communion; 3. Lord's table; 4. Lord's supper; 5. remembrance, me; 6. Eucharist, action, grace) Did you get them? Very good. Without doubt each name has its significance and thought and deeper instruction. In our study here we are not going to consider how the Lord Jesus Christ presented (makes Himself present at . . .) the Lord's Table. (See the note on this item at the end of this lesson, Question 1.) The fact is that He is present at the Supper with true believers meeting in His name. Jesus is _____ at the Lord's Supper.

121. (present) We note that Jesus is the center of the meeting and that the Table, the Supper belongs to Him. It is the Lord's. We believe that the Lord Jesus instituted two ordinances: baptism and the Lord's Table. The principal passages about the Lord's Supper are: Matt. 26:26-30; Mark 14:22-26; Luke 22:14-20; Acts 2:42-46; Acts 20:7; I Cor. 10:16-21; I Cor. 11:23-34. It is clear that it would be very profitable to study each passage. But our study is limited! In the passages of the Gospels (Matt., Mark, Luke) we find these words: "And as they were eating Jesus took bread, blessed it and broke it, and gave it to the disciples and said, 'Take, eat; this is My body.'" (Matt. 26:26) Luke adds these words ". . . which is given for you; do this in remembrance of Me." He who instituted the Lord's Supper was _____.

122. (Jesus) That is so! Jesus celebrated the first Supper with His disciples. It was Jesus who _____ the Lord's Supper.

123. (instituted) The practice continued in the churches of the New Testament. Read I Cor. 11:23-32. Have you read it? Very good. In this passage we have the instruction that Paul gave to the Corinthian church. This is a passage full of teaching, significance, warning--and blessing. Let us notice some of the precious things in this passage. We won't pretend to make a complete or comprehensive study. In I Cor. 11:23, Paul writes,

"For I received from the Lord that which I also delivered to you." Paul received this instruction from the _____.

124. (Lord) That's right! Paul received this teaching from the Lord Jesus. But He did not keep it only to himself. He _____ the teaching to the believers in Corinth.

125. (delivered) He delivered the teaching to the believers. Now, this teaching begins with the word "for" in verse 23, "For I received from the Lord." The one who gave the teaching to Paul was the _____.

126. (Lord) ". . . the Lord Jesus on the same night in which He was betrayed took bread." Jesus was betrayed on Passover night. Jesus instituted the Lord's Supper on the night of the last _____.

127. (Passover) Jesus was betrayed by _____.

128. (Judas) On that night Jesus instituted the _____ _____.

129. (Lord's Supper) Jesus took bread, gave thanks, and broke it and said: "This is My body, which is given for you; do this in remembrance of me." Jesus commanded, "_____ this."

130. (do) When we take the bread we should do it in remembrance of _____.

131. (Jesus) In I Cor. 11, verse 25, Jesus took the cup. He said: "This cup is the new covenant in My blood." The cup represents the _____ testament (covenant) in the _____ of Jesus.

132. (new, blood) Again Jesus says: "Do this." It is the will of Jesus that we celebrate the Lord's Supper. It is a command of Jesus. Jesus _____ that we celebrate the Lord's Supper.

133. (commanded) It is a memorial feast. Jesus says, "Do this in _____ of _____."

134. (remembrance, Me) Verse 26 explains a precious and important truth. It says, "For as often as you eat this bread and drink this cup, you proclaim the Lord's death till He comes." Paul teaches us that this feast preaches (announces, proclaims) the death of _____.

135. (Jesus) His death is the basis of our salvation. Jesus died for our sins. His death is a basic fact of the Gospel. When the congregation takes the Lord's Supper "in spirit and truth," it is preaching the _____.

136. (Gospel) This is true: the bread and the cup represent (among other things) the death of the _____.

137. (Lord) The passage also says, "Until He comes." This speaks of the Second Coming of the Lord. We should celebrate the Lord's Supper until the _____ coming of _____.

138. (Second, Jesus) The one who instituted the Lord's Supper was this same _____.

139. (Jesus) There are various names used for the Lord's Supper. Look again at item 119. The fact is that Jesus is _____ at the Lord's Supper or Table.

140. (present) The Apostle Paul received teaching concerning the Supper from the Lord _____.

141. (Jesus) In the passage in I Cor. 11:23-26, the bread and the cup represent the _____ of _____.

142. (death, Jesus) In celebrating the Lord's Supper the believers proclaim the Lord's death until the _____ _____.

143. (Second Coming)

Suggestions and Plans for the Group Study

Lesson 6: The Lord's Table

Plan:

1. Be sure the students have already studied the lesson or reserve time for the study.

2. Read passages related to the subject.

3. Use the following questions or references to motivate the exchange of ideas.

Questions and References:

1. What are the names used for the Lord's Table? Discuss more deeply the significance of each name.

2. What is the significance of the Lord's Table to Jesus Himself?

3. How are believers able to realize or experience the presence of the Lord at the Table?

4. What is the significance of John 4:23,24 in relationship to the Lord's Table?

5. What is the significance of the last Passover?

LESSON 7   THE LORD'S TABLE (SUPPER):
WARNING AND FREQUENCY OF CELEBRATION

Upon finishing this lesson, the student should be able to:

--Explain the importance of I Cor. 11:27-32.

--Tell of the privilege the believer has of examining himself.

--Express thoughts about the Lord's Table as a meeting of the church.

--Understand the convictions of some regarding the frequency of celebrating the Lord's Table.

144. There is much yet that can be studied in these verses (I Cor. 11:23-26). Verses 27 and 29 are an important and serious warning. They say, "Therefore whoever eats . . . in an unworthy manner (unworthily) will be guilty of the body and blood of the Lord." And "For he who eats and drinks in an unworthy manner (unworthily) eats and drinks judgment to himself, not discerning the Lord's body." These verses are a serious _____.

145. (warning) Some of the Corinthians were taking the Lord's Table in an unworthy manner or unworthily and without discernment. They were guilty and worthy of judgment! The carnal believers of the Corinthian church took the Lord's Table unworthily. They were _____.

146. (guilty) The result of their actions, of their sin and lack of being spiritual, is found in verse 30, ". . . weak and sick among you, and many sleep." It can be seen that these words refer to their physical states--weak, sickly and death! ("sin brings death"). But it is more certain that they refer to a spiritual state: spiritual weakness, spiritual sickness, spiritual death! Among the Corinthians believers some were "_____ and _____ . . . and many _____."

147. (weak, sickly, sleep) What should be done then? In verses 28, 31, 32, we find precious truths and privileges. To take the Lord's Table and thus express our fellowship and union with Christ, our remembrance of His death, our discernment of His body, is a very serious act. For this reason, the Apostle wrote, ". . . Let a man examine himself." It is an obligation and responsibility for every believer to _____ _____.

148. (examine himself) The believer ought to examine himself before partaking of the Lord's Table. In I Cor. 11:31 we read, "If we judge ourselves." The two words used are _____ and _____.

149. (examine, judge) The believer has the right and privilege to examine and judge himself. He should examine himself to see if there is any sin in his

life: pride, immorality, critical spirit, hatred or resentment with another brother, jealousy, envy, lying, stealing, etc. He judges that it is sin and confesses it before partaking of the Lord's Table. (See I John 1:9 and 2:1). The believer has the privilege of _____ _____ and _____ _____.

150. (examining himself, judging himself) And Paul wrote, ". . . And so let him eat of that bread and drink of that cup." The believer is to judge the sin in order to return immediately to full fellowship with Christ and other believers. Therefore, the believer should always maintain fellowship with _____, and with other _____ in Christ.

151. (Christ, believers) This fellowship is expressed by celebrating the _____ _____.

152. (Lord's Table) The promise for the believer that judges himself is, "we would not be judged." The believer that judges himself is not _____.

153. (judged) But, when we do not judge ourselves, then the Lord has to discipline us as sons: "But when we are judged, we are chastened by the Lord." The Lord loves us and for this reason he _____ us.

154. (chastens) The reason for this chastening (discipline) is "that we may not be condemned with the world." (See Romans 8:1.) The believer should _____ _____ and _____ _____ before taking the Lord's Table.

155. (examine himself, judge himself) This is a great _____ and blessing.

156. (privilege or responsibility) We have considered the third activity of the church, "The breaking of bread." Now we wish to study the question, How frequently should we celebrate the Lord's Table? The question that we want to consider is with what _____ we should celebrate the _____ _____.

157. (frequency, Lord's Table) Should we celebrate the Lord's Table each month, every three months, once a year or each week? Much depends upon whether we consider the Lord's Table as a <u>meeting of the church</u> or only as an important spiritual feast that we celebrate once in awhile. What was <u>the</u> meeting of the church in the times of the apostles? Let us consider whether the Lord's Table is a _____ of the _____ or a _____ once in awhile.

158. (meeting, church, celebration) The Apostle Paul expresses a meeting of the church in this form: "When you come together as a church,"--I Cor. 11:18; "therefore, when you come together in one place," I Cor. 11:20. "How is it then, brethren? Whenever you come together, each of you has a psalm, has a teaching, has a tongue, has a revelation, has an interpretation, let all things be done for edification," I Cor. 14:26. The phrase repeated is, "_____ you _____ _____."

159. (When, come together) There was a meeting of the believers to exercise the gifts of I Cor. 12 and 14 with the foundation of love expressed in I Cor. 13. Paul says (in the previous item), "let all things be done for _____."

160. (edification) At this time they also celebrated the Lord's Supper. It may be that the teachings of I Cor. 10:14-22 and I Cor. 11,12,13,14 are in the context of the Lord's Supper as the main meeting of the church. It seems that the Lord's Supper is the _____ of the _____.

161. (meeting, church) The main meeting of the church, the meeting for adoration or the worship service, is the _____ _____.

162. (Lord's Supper) If the Lord's Supper is a meeting, with what frequency

should we celebrate it? In Acts 2:46 we read, ". . . breaking bread from house to house, they ate their food with gladness and simplicity of heart." If this "breaking of bread" is the Lord's Supper, then it seems that the Lord's Supper was celebrated almost every day. It is possible in the beginning that they celebrated the Lord's Supper almost _____ _____.

163. (every day) In Acts 20:7 we read: "Now on the first day of the week, when the disciples came together to break bread." (vs. 11, "had broken bread and eaten,"). In this passage the believers of Troas celebrated the Lord's Supper with the Apostle _____.

164. (Paul) They celebrated this meeting of adoration on the _____ day of the _____.

165. (first, week) The first day of the week is _____.

166. (Sunday) Even though this verse does not say with what frequency they celebrated the Lord's Table, it does say that they were meeting with the purpose of _____ _____ on the _____ day of the _____.

50

167. (breaking bread, first, week) In John 20:19 and 26, we find these words, "Then, the same day at evening, being the first day of the week, . . . Jesus came and stood in the midst, and said to them, 'Peace be with you.'" "And after eight days His disciples were again inside . . . Jesus came . . . and stood in the midst . . . ." Jesus came on the _____ day of the _____ and also _____ days later.

168. (first, week, eight) Now this fact doesn't have anything to do with the Lord's Supper precisely! We only wish to note that Jesus was with His disciples two _____ together and that they had fellowship and gladness together.

169. (Sundays) Another important passage concerning the question of frequency is I Cor. 11:26, "For as often as you eat this bread and drink this cup." Here we note that it doesn't say how many times but says, "_____ _____ _____."

170. (as often as) Regarding this thought, there seems to be much liberty as to the frequency of celebration. "As often as" could be many times or each time, but it does express the idea, "frequently." The passage expresses that we should celebrate the Lord's Table _____.

171. (frequently) Let us notice something of this frequency in the history of the church. In the second century there is a writing which is called, <u>The Teachings of the Twelve Apostles</u>. In this writing it says that they celebrated the Lord's Supper "Every Lord's Day." There seems to be evidence that they celebrated the Lord's Supper "_____ _____ _____" or each week (Sunday).

172. (Every Lord's Day) In the history of groups that have returned to the simplicity of the Word of God, they began celebrating the Lord's Table every Sunday. We cite the following groups: the Baptists (Ana-Baptists), the Methodists, Presbyterians, Waldensens, Plymouth Brethren. There is historical evidence of groups that celebrated the Lord's Table every _____.

173. (week or Sunday) We find in the teachings of John Wesley that he personally celebrated the Lord's Supper every three days and taught his followers that they should do this every week. John Wesley taught that the Lord's Supper ought to be celebrated every _____.

174. (week) John Calvin taught that the Lord's Supper should be celebrated at least once a week. According to him the communion should be celebrated at least _____ week.

175. (each) What then is our conclusion? The conclusion is that the Lord's Supper should be celebrated each week. The Lord's Supper is a _____ of the _____.

176. (meeting, church) The Lord's Supper should be celebrated at least each _____.

177. (week or Lord's Day) This, of course, does not suggest that those who celebrate the Lord's Supper once a month or less frequently are not "worshiping the Lord" at that time! They are obeying the word, "As often as."

Suggestions and Plan for the Group Study:

Lesson 7: The Lord's Table; Warning and Frequency

PLAN:

1. Be sure the students have already studied the lesson or reserve time for the study.

2. Read passages related to the subject.

3. Use the following questions or references to motivate the exchange of ideas.

Questions:

1. What is the importance of the believer examining himself before taking the Lord's Supper?

2. What is the privilege that the believer has that the unbeliever doesn't have?

3. Is the Lord's Table a celebration that is done once in awhile or is it a meeting of the church? What do you think?

4. With what frequency should we celebrate the Lord's Table?

LESSON 8   THE PRAYER MEETING

Upon finishing this lesson, the student should be able to:

--Explain the importance of the church prayer meeting.

--Give thoughts of Jesus' teachings about prayer.

--Show to others the place of prayer in the first local church.

178. We have studied the perseverance of the church in Jerusalem as an example of a local church. In Acts 2:42, the Scriptures say, "and they continued steadfastly in the apostles' doctrine and fellowship, in breaking of bread, and in _____."

179. (prayers) Prayer is one of the two most important things in the believer's life and in the life of the local church. The believer that does not pray will be weak. The church that does not pray also will be ____.

180. (weak) We note that the Jerusalem church "persevered" in _____.

181. (prayer) Now we are going to study the importance of the prayer meeting in the life of the church. It would be good first of all to return to the words of Jesus in Matt. 18:15-20. In verse 17, we have seen that the word "church" is repeated two times. The content then speaks in regard

to the _____.

182. (church) This is the local church in prayer. We read in verse 19 and 20, "again I say to you, that if two of you agree on earth concerning any thing that they ask, it will be done for them by my Father in Heaven. For where there are two or more gathered in my name, I am there in the midst of them." We have already studied (lesson 2, items 27-30) that these verses are speaking about the _____ _____ in _____.

183. (local church, prayer) Also in verse 20 we have noted the promise of the _____ of _____.

184. (presence, Jesus) This presence of Jesus is in the context of a _____ meeting.

185. (prayer) Jesus is present in the prayer meeting. We refer to the words of Alexander R. Hay (<u>Field news</u>, August, 1974, pp. 117): "He Himself is present in the midst with His power, wisdom, and divine, and absolute authority . . . He is present with those that are meeting in His name, as a functioning church, . . . even thought there are only two or three." Now we come to note the word, "for." This word refers to verse 19 where we find the two or three agreeing in prayer. These two or three

represent the simplest _____ _____, and not any two in whatever place.

186. (local, church) Here we note the local church in unanimous prayer. The agreeing here is not of a majority of votes but of an agreement together of all the members of the church. The local church should be _____ in prayer.

187. (unanimous) This agreeing or being unanimous in regard to whatever might be asked is possible because Jesus is _____.

188. (present) The local church is agreeing with the Lord Jesus because He is in the midst of them. This is agreeing with the will of God. The two or three (the simplest church) are to agree with the _____ of God.

189. (will) Also in verse 19 there is a great promise. It is the promise of answered prayer in the local church. It is expressed in these words: " it will be done for them by _____ _____ in _____.

190. (My Father, heaven) What a blessing! When we are met together and unanimous with Christ in prayer, the Father answers our petitions. The church in prayer has the promise of _____ to prayer from the

_____.

191. (answers, Father) We wish to note some other words of the Lord Jesus about prayer. For example, in John 14:13,14, Jesus said, "And whatever you ask in My name, that I will do, that the Father may be glorified in the Son. If you ask anything in My name, I will do it." When we pray, we should ask in the name of _____.

192. (Jesus) Yes. We should pray in the name of Jesus Christ. Two times we find the words, ". . . in My name." Two times we find the promise of Jesus "I _____ _____ it."

193. (will do) The purpose of asking prayer in the name of Jesus is "that the _____ may be _____ in the Son."

194. (Father, glorified) Let us make a list of conditions necessary in order that the believer or the church may receive answers to their prayers:
    1. The believer needs to abide in Christ. (Jn. 15:7)
    2. He needs to be walking in accordance with the Word of God. (I John 3:22)
    3. His prayer needs to be in accordance with the Word of God. (Matt. 22:29)

4. His prayer needs to be in accordance with God's will. (I Jn. 5:14,15)

5. Answers depend on his attitude to those around him. (Matt. 5:23,24; Mark 11:24,25; I Tim. 2:8)

6. His prayer should be "in the Spirit." (Eph. 6:18; Jude 20; Rom. 8:26,27)

7. He should pray with faith, a faith given by the Spirit for that which is in the will of God. (Mark 11:24; I Cor. 12:9; James 1:7-8)

In order to receive answers to prayer there are certain _____.

195. (conditions) Let us note something about the first church in prayer. In a real and true sense the church began in a prayer meeting. In Acts 1:13,14 and 2:1-4 we read, "and when they had entered, they went up into the upper room . . . These all continued with one accord in prayer and supplication . . . Now when the Day of Pentecost had fully come, they were all with one accord in one place. And suddenly there came a sound from heaven, as of a rushing mighty wind, and it filled the whole house where they were sitting . . . And they were all filled with the Holy Spirit . . . ." In a real and true sense the church began on the day of Pentecost in a _____ _____.

196. (prayer meeting) The church began in a prayer meeting. But did they continue praying? We have already noted in Acts 2:42 that, yes, they did. "And they continued steadfastly . . . in prayers." The first local church continued in _____.

197. (prayer) But how did the church face its problems? One problem that arose immediately was persecution. Peter and John were imprisoned and were prohibited to speak anymore in the name of Jesus. Let us notice what happened (4:23,24): "And being let go, they went to their own companions and reported all that the chief priests and elders had said to them. So when they heard that, they raised their voice to God with one accord." When there are problems among believers in the congregation or with the testimony, the brethren should gather for _____.

198. (prayer) Also in verse 24, we note, "So when they heard that, raised their voice to God with _____ _____."

199. (one accord) A church having a problem should unite together to pray. What was the result of this unanimity in prayer? In 4:31, we read, "And when they had prayed, the place where they were assembled together was shaken and they were all filled with the Holy Spirit, and they spake the Word of God with boldness." God gave a wonderful answer to their

_____.

200. (prayers) In Acts 12:5, Peter was imprisoned again, "but constant prayer was offered to God for him by the church." We can say that whenever a brother or sister is in whatever danger the church should _____ for him.

201. (pray) The church was growing and spreading, not only among the Jews but also among the Gentiles. "Now in the church that was at Antioch there were certain prophets and teachers . . . As they ministered to the Lord and fasted, the Holy Spirit said, 'Separate to Me Barnabus and Saul for the work to which I have called them.' Then having fasted and prayed, and laid hands on them, they sent them away," (Acts 13:1-3. We notice another occasion for prayer. When the church was growing and God wished to use certain members to expand the work, He revealed His will and calling to all who were in _____.

202. (prayer) These brethren were sincere and serious. The Word says that they not only prayed but they also _____.

203. (fasted) Yes. Sometimes it is necessary that the church pass time in prayer and fasting in order to know and do the will of God. In fact, all

61

the activities of the church should be done with much _____.

204. (prayer) Later, when Paul was traveling and preaching the Gospel and congregations were established, there was need for leaders in the churches. What should they do? In Acts 14:23, we read, "So when they had appointed elders in every church, and prayed with fasting, they commended them to the Lord in whom they had believed." In the election of local church officers there is need of much _____.

205. (prayer) That's true! In every decision of the church, there should be unanimity in prayer. Let us note only three other passages concerning prayer. We find one in Acts 20:36. Paul is with the elders of the Ephesian church, and having said good-bye to them for the last time, all were sad--but we read, "And when he had said these things, he knelt down and prayed with them all." (See also 21:5.) In difficult and emotional times, the brethren prayed together. All of us need the blessing of God in prayer together in _____ and _____ times such as good-byes.

206. (difficult, emotional) Another very important passage is James 5:13-17. Read these verses in your Bible. In these verses, how many times do we find the word "prayer" or "to pray?"

a. 4 times

b. 5 times

c. 6 times

d. 7 times

207. (d) An example of a man that prayed with faith and fervency was _____.

208. (Elijah) There is a lot of teaching in this passage which we will not consider now. But one question. What should an ill or sick person in the congregation do? Notice verse 14. He should ____ the _____ of the _____.

209. (call, elders, church) In these verses, then, when there is suffering (vs. 13), sickness (vs. 14) or sin (vs. 16) the brethren of the church need to _____.

210. (pray) Now we all know that prayer is a battle field. Many times as individual believers or as churches we do not dedicate sufficient time in prayer. But Paul teaches us the importance of winning the battle. We read in Eph. 6:18,19, "Praying always with all prayer and supplication in the Spirit, being watchful to this end with all perseverance and

supplication for all the saints--And for me, that utterance may be given to me, that I may open my mouth boldly to make known the mystery of the Gospel." What a marvelous and instructive passage! See if you can fill in the words that are lacking. In verse 18:

". . . All _____ and _____ . . . in the Spirit, . . . with all _____ and supplication for all of the _____ ."

211. (prayer, supplication, perseverance, saints) The church in Jerusalem "persevered in _____ ."

212. (prayers) The local church needs to keep its _____ _____ .

213. (prayer meeting) The prayer meeting has the promise of the _____ of Jesus.

214. (presence) The words "one accord" express the thought that the local church should have _____ in prayer.

215. (unanimity) The church is agreeing or seeking unanimity with the _____ of God.

216. (will)

Suggestions and Plan for the Group Study:

Lesson 8: The Prayer Meeting

Plan:

1. Be sure the students have already studied the lesson or reserve time for the study.

2. Read passages related to the subject.

3. Use the following question for references to motivate the exchange of ideas.

Questions and References:

1. How do you apply Matt. 18:19,20, to the prayer meeting?

2. What are the conditions necessary in the life of the believer in order to receive answers from his prayers? (see item 194)

3. What is the importance of prayer in the growth of the church?

4. Are the words of James 5:14 practical in your church?

5. Why does it say that prayer is a battle field?

LESSON 9 THE BODY OF CHRIST:

THE MANIFESTATIONS OF THE HOLY SPIRIT

Upon finishing this lesson, the student should be able to:

--Explain something about the Body of Christ and its members.

--Define the gifts of the Spirit.

--Tell why God gave gifts to the members of the church.

217. In our studies we have dedicated a lot of time to the activities of the first local church and its application to our day. We have seen the vital life of the functioning church according to New Testament norms. But the church, the Body of Christ, is composed of members, all saints. In I Peter 2:5 we read, "You also, as living stones, are being built up a spiritual house, a holy priesthood." Also in verse 9, "But you are a chosen generation, a royal priesthood." In Revelation 1:5-6, we read what Jesus did for our redemption ". . . Unto Him who loved us and washed us from our sins in His own blood, and has made us kings and priests unto His God and His Father . . . ." Every member of the church, every believer is a _____.

218. (priest) A priest has privileges and responsibilities for ministry. All believers in the church have _____ and _____ as priests.

219. (privileges, responsibilities) God made the members of the body interdependent. (See in I Corinthians 12:12-17, the vital unity of the church) As it says in verse 12, "For as the body is one and has many members, but the members of that one body, being many, are one body, so also is Christ." And verse 27, "Now you are the body of Christ, and members individually." The Body has many _____.

220. (members) Yes. There are many members but only one _____.

221. (Body) Therefore every believer is a member of the Body of Christ, a priest with privileges and responsibilities. Now God gave <u>gifts</u> or <u>manifestations or capacities</u> of the Spirit for the better functioning of the Body. Yes. God gave _____ or _____ or _____ of the Spirit in order that the Body might function well.

222. (gifts, manifestations, capacities) There are several important passages relating to the subject of the <u>gifts</u> and <u>ministries</u> or <u>capacities</u> given by the Holy Spirit to believers for ministry, Romans 12:3-8; I Corinthians 12:1-11; 27-31; Chapter 14; Ephesians 4:7-16; I Peter 4:10-11. We do not pretend to study in detail each passage. First, let's look at the list that we find in Ephesians 4:11, "And He Himself gave some to be <u>apostles</u>, some <u>prophets</u>, some <u>evangelists</u>, and some <u>pastors</u> and <u>teachers</u>." Make a list

of the ministries in this passage:

1. _____   2. _____

3. _____   4. _____

5. _____

223. (apostles, prophets, evangelists, pastors, teachers) These ministries are the <u>basic</u> or <u>fundamental</u> ministries (capacities) in the church of Christ. Three out of five of these we have in I Corinthians 12:28, <u>apostles</u>, <u>prophets</u>, and <u>teachers</u>. These ministries are the _____ or _____ ministries of the church.

224. (basic, fundamental) It is important to distinguish between: 1. Spiritual gifts, 2. Spiritual fruit (I Cor. 13, Gal. 5:22,23) and 3. Spiritual positions or functions. The five basic ministries are treated more as spiritual _____.

225. (positions or functions) Yes, the five basic ministries have to do more with the spiritual composition of leadership in the church. In our study now, let us consider more the question of the spiritual gifts. In I Cor. 12:1, we read, "Now concerning spiritual gifts, brethren, I do not want you to be ignorant." It seems that in the Corinthian church there was _____ in regard to the spiritual gifts.

226. (ignorance) Yes, Paul wrote, "I do not want you to be ignorant." There was ignorance in those days and also today there is much confusion regarding the gifts or manifestations of the Spirit. We do not wish to be _____.

227. (ignorant) First of all, we wish to note a very important thing. In I Cor. 12:7, we read, "But the manifestations of the Spirit is given to each one for the profit of all." And in Eph. 4:7, "But unto each one of us grace was given according to the measure of Christ's gift." These passages declare that he manifestations or gifts of the Spirit are to _____ _____.

228. (each one) Yes, each believer has a gift or gifts of the Holy Spirit. These gifts are manifestations, functions (Rom. 12:4) or spiritual capacities. All are members of the Body of Christ and the manifestations of the Spirit are given to _____ _____.

229. (each one) Let's look now at the lists of the spiritual gifts given in Scripture. Read Rom. 12:3-8. Did you read it? Perhaps the best way will be to list the gifts and give a short explanation of each one. Paul writes in verse 6, "Having then gifts differing according to the grace that is given to us, let us use them: if prophecy, let us prophesy in proportion to our faith." This is the gift of prophecy (see I Cor. 14:3), or preaching the

message of God. The preaching of truth is revealed in the power and demonstration of the Spirit; and it should be in proportion to our faith. The first gift here is the gift of _____ or _____.

230. (prophecy, preaching) In verse 7, we read, "Or <u>ministry</u>, let us use it in our ministering." In other translations we find the words, "to serve," "to be of service," and "they should serve well." Now the ministry can be spiritual and material. Without doubt some are going to say that this is the ministry, in the professional sense, but in the context, the gifts do not have this meaning. If it is material, the service is done under the direction of the Holy Spirit. (See the spiritual ministry in the life of Jesus in Mark 10:45). The second gift mentioned is the gift of _____.

231. (ministry) Yes, this ministry is to serve others by the grace of the Holy Spirit. The third gift we also find in verse 7, "he who <u>teaches</u> in teaching." This is the gift of teaching the Word of God, the teaching of spiritual things with wisdom and light given by the Spirit. If anyone has this gift, he should dedicate himself in doing it. This gift of _____ is very important in the church.

232. (teaching) In verse 8, we have number four of the gifts in this passage, " or <u>he who exhorts</u> in exhortation." This is the gift of the paraclete, to

"come alongside," to encourage others. It is a very necessary and delicate gift. To give counseling, encouragement, and even reproof must be inspired by the Holy Spirit, manifesting the pure love and wisdom of Christ. If you, brother or sister, have this gift, "do it with dedication." The gift of giving encouragement, etc. is the gift of _____.

233. (exhortation) The next gift, number 5, is, "He who gives with liberality," or with generosity, or simplicity. Another thought is, "he who shares with others that which he has." This is the gift of giving. Every believer should give under the guidance of the Spirit, but it is possible that some have more "means" than others and the special gift of giving with liberality or generosity. This is the gift of _____.

234. (giving or contributing) Another gift in verse 8 is, "he who leads, with diligence;" with care or seriousness. Other words that help us to understand this gift are: to govern, to have authority or capacity of administration, that is, presiding or governing under the control and direction of the Holy Spirit. How necessary these gifts are! Very important is the gift of _____ or _____.

235. (presiding, governing) Another gift is, "he who shews mercy, with cheerfulness." This gift is for showing love to others, to console those

sorrowing or discouraged, and to help others to manifest the love of Christ by the Spirit. How many times we attempt to do these things because we ought to and not "with joy." What a precious gift is the gift or manifestation of _____.

236. (mercy) Good! Here in Romans we have noted seven gifts. Now let's come to I Cor. 12:7-11. We have already seen that every believer has a gift and it is his obligation to exercise his gift. In verse 8, we read, "For to one is given the <u>word of wisdom</u> through the Spirit, to another the <u>word of knowledge</u> the same Spirit." Here we have two gifts. Let's consider the first. This is the message of wisdom given by the Spirit. It is "clarity in the declaration of spiritual truths revealed" (Hay). It seems that there are not many who have the gift of the _____ of _____.

237. (word, wisdom) The other gift here is the "<u>word of knowledge</u>." One thought is that it is the believer who is able to study and teach. Alex. R. Hay suggests that it is the "application of spiritual truth in the practical experiences of life under the inspiration of the Spirit." The difference between these gifts seems to be: one is the declaration of truth and the other is the application of the truth. The two seem to be connected to the gift of teaching. This gift is the _____ of _____.

238. (word, knowledge) In verse 9, we read, "To another <u>faith</u> by the same Spirit; to another gifts of healings by the same Spirit." Let us consider the gift of faith. This is not the faith for salvation that all true believers possess and which they receive from God (Eph. 2:8,9). This is a special faith given by the Spirit according to the Word of God and His will. Examples in recent history could be the faith of George Mueller of England or of Hudson Taylor, missionary to China. Without doubt there are many others who have this gift. In the Body of Christ it is necessary that all the gifts be manifested including the gift of _____.

239. (faith) The other gift mentioned in verse 9 is "<u>the gifts of healings</u>." These gifts of healing are done by the power of God in answer to faith according to His will. The Biblical instructions regarding sickness is found in James 5:14, "Is anyone among you sick? Let him call for the elders of the church . . . . " Very important in the church are the _____ of _____.

240. (gifts, healing) Now in I Cor. 12:10 we find five more gifts! We read, "to another the <u>working of miracles</u>, to another <u>prophecy</u>; to another <u>discerning of spirits</u>; to another <u>different kinds of tongues</u>; to another the <u>interpretation of tongues</u>." Miracles! In the first church there were many miracles done by the apostles. They are the "direct intervention of divine

power in response to faith that is given by the Holy Spirit for that which is in accordance with the will of God" (Hay). Without doubt the necessity of this gift depends much on the conditions of society and in the plan and purpose of God. The first gift in this verse is the _____ of _____.

241. (working, miracles) Another gift to consider is "<u>discernment of spirits</u>" or the capacity of knowing the difference between gifts that come from the Spirit and those that do not. It is to discern if they are from evil spirits or the Spirit of God. A gift that seems very necessary in our days is the gift of _____ of _____.

242. (discernment, spirits) The other two gifts deal with the question of tongues. The first is "<u>kinds of tongues</u>" or unknown tongues. These are living languages such as were expressed on the Day of Pentecost as a sign to unbelievers. They have the purpose of carrying the message of God. On the day of Pentecost they were "known tongues." There is absolutely no evidence of "ecstatic" tongues. The gift in much evidence on the day of Pentecost was _____ of _____.

243. (kinds, tongues) The gift that is the "companion" of "kinds of tongues" is the "<u>interpretation of tongues</u>." In the "interpretation," it is not

necessary that the interpreter not know the language or tongue spoken or that the interpretation is unknown by the interpreter. A present application is expressed in these words by Alex. R. Hay, "Guidance given by the Spirit for the interpretation or translation of the Word of God, whether in written form or spoken, of one language to another." The gift that is the "companion" of kinds of tongues is _____ of _____. I Cor. 14 teaches us in detail how to use these gifts. (See number two of the questions)

244. (interpretation, tongues) In this list in Corinthians, there are nine gifts mentioned. (See also I Peter 4:8-11.) One is repeated in Romans, that of prophecy. A comparison of the two lists shows that there are something like fifteen gifts or manifestations of the Spirit. Paul teaches us that there are at least _____ gifts to be used.

245. (fifteen) But what is the good or purpose of these gifts? Paul teaches us that they are "for the profit or for the good of all." He also uses the word "edification." The gifts are for the profit, the good, the edification, of each believer and the growth of the church. ("In order that the church might receive edification"). Notice this word in I Cor. 14:12, "Even so you, since you are zealous for spiritual gifts, let it be for the edification of the church that you seek to excel." Yes. The purpose of the gifts is the

of the church that you seek to excel." Yes. The purpose of the gifts is the _____, the _____, and the _____ of the church.

246. (profit, good, edification) In the church of Christ all the members are _____ with privileges and responsibilities. (See items 217.)

247. (saints) In the church, the Body of Christ, there are many _____.

248. (members) For the better functioning of the church, God gave _____ or _____, _____. or _____ to the church. (See items 221 and 222.)

249. (gifts, manifestations, ministries, capacities) In your own words, why did God give the gifts of the Spirit? _____.

250. (In order that the church could function better or for the profit, the good, and the edification of the church or for the well being of the church and its growth, or similar words.)

Suggestions and Plan for the Group Study:

Lesson 9: The Gifts or Manifestations of the Spirit

Plan:

1. Be sure the students have already studied the lesson or reserve time for the study.

2. Read passages related to the subject.

3. Use the following questions or references to motivate the exchange of ideas.

Questions and References:

1. What are the basic ministries and their importance in the church?

2. What are the gifts of the Spirit? What is your gift or gifts?

3. What is the purpose of the gifts?

4. Discuss the concepts: Discovering your gift; Developing your gift; Using your gift.

5. What are the other <u>figures</u> used to illustrate the Body of Christ? Study:
    1. the Shepherd and the sheep (John 10).
    2. the Vine and the branches (John 15).
    3. the Cornerstone and the stones of the building (Eph. 2:19-21).
    4. the High Priest and a kingdom of priests (I Peter 2).
    5. the Head and the Body (I Cor. 12).
    6. the Last Adam and the new creation (Rom. 5).
    7. the Bridegroom and the Bride (Eph. 5).

    (<u>The Ryrie Study Bible</u>, p. 1952)

LESSON 10 THE OFFICES OR POSITIONS IN THE LOCAL CHURCH: ELDERS (PRESBYTERS, BISHOPS, PASTORS) AND DEACONS

Upon finishing this lesson, the student will be able to

--Name the two offices in the local church.

--Give the other names for presbyter.

--Explain something of the plurality of presbyters and deacons.

--Verify the ministry of the deacon.

251. We have studied regarding the members of the Body of Christ, the members of the local church, and the fact that each member has a gift or gifts that should be used for the edification of the Body. In the organization of the local church, the Bible also teaches us that there are "officials." The two officials in the local church are the presbyter and the deacon. Now let us study concerning the _____ of the church.

252. (officials) In the government of the local church, there are two offices or positions: the _____ and the _____.

253. (presbyter, deacon) Let's consider, first of all, the presbyter. There are

three other words in the New Testament: elder, bishop, pastor. Are these four different people? In order to identify these names, let us note the verses in Acts 20:17 and 28 "From Miletus he sent to Ephesus, and called for the <u>elders</u> of the church . . . (the <u>presbyters</u>) . . . therefore take heed to yourselves and to all the flock, among which the Holy Spirit has made you <u>overseers</u> (or <u>bishops</u>) to <u>shepherd</u> the church of God which He purchased with His own blood." The four names cited above are: _____ or _____, _____, _____.

254. (elders or presbyters, overseers or bishops) There is also the verb "to shepherd,"the work of a pastor. In the context and in other biblical passages it seems well established that these five names signify the same person. The five names: presbyters, elders, overseers, bishops, pastors signify only one _____.

255. (person) Yes. There is evidence that these are not five different persons or different positions, but indicate that they are different functions or responsibilities of the same position or office. The first two names are _____ and _____.

256. (presbyter, elder) It seems that these names indicate the office or place

of the person's ministry. The person is a _____ or an _____.

257. (presbyter, elder) Yes, the person is a presbyter or elder. Now his ministry or responsibility is as a bishop (overseer, supervisor, shepherd, pastor) who guards and takes care of the sheep or flock. The ministry or work of the presbyter is as a _____ or _____ or _____.

258. (bishop, overseer, pastor) While we are here in verse 28, let us note two precious and important things. The verse says, "Therefore take heed unto yourselves and to all the flock, among which the Holy Spirit has made you overseers. . . ." He who made or set aside these men for their offices, positions or responsibilities was the _____ _____.

259. (Holy Spirit) Yes. How important is this concept! It is the Holy Spirit who prepares and calls men for their ministry. The choice is from Him and not from men, although the other believers (the church) must recognize the call and the preparation. Let us remember that the true call to be a presbyter is from the _____ _____.

260. (Holy Spirit) This is true. The Holy Spirit is He who chooses His

officials in the Body of Christ. One other thing here are the words, ". . . the church of God which He purchased with His own blood." Here we have the value of the church in the eyes of God. He bought His people with the highest price--His ____ _____.

261. (own blood) How wonderful! God bought us with His own blood! How we should have and feel great gratitude. What responsibility the leaders of the church have! God loves His church (His people) because He bought her with ____ own _____.

262. (His, blood) Now in verse 17 we have already noted, ". . . he sent . . . and called for the elders (or presbyters) of the church." Presbyters or elders are in the plural of the noun (more than one). Let us study the concept of the plurality of the presbyters (elders, bishops, pastors). Read Phil. 1:1, "Paul and Timothy, servants of Jesus Christ, to all the saints in Christ Jesus who are in Philippi, with the bishops and deacons." The words underlined are: (circle the correct letter)

   a. in the singular.
   b. in the plural.

263. (b) Yes. They are in the plural, which means that there were more than one bishop and one deacon. In Acts 14:23, we read, "So when they had

appointed <u>elders</u> in every church." The word underlined is: (choose one)

   a.   in the plural.

   b.   in the singular.

264.   (a) Read Titus 1:5, "For this reason I left you in Crete, that you should set in order the things that are lacking, and appoint <u>elders</u> in every city." The word underlined is: (circle the correct letter)

   a.   in the singular.

   b.   in the plural.

265.   (b) Yes. In the plural. There is no evidence whatsoever in the New Testament of having only one presbyter (elder, bishop, pastor) over one local church. There is always a plurality. It is the Biblical order! And without doubt there are many reasons why this is so! In the wisdom of God, there is protection against many abuses that could arise in having only one person with authority in the congregation. There is in the local church always a _____ of presbyters and deacons.

266.   (plurality) In the organization of the local church there are two positions: the _____ and the _____.

267.   (presbyters, deacons) The other names used for the presbyters are:

_____, _____, _____ or

_____.

268. (elders, bishops, overseers, pastors) There are always a plurality of pastors in the local church. Let us now consider the second position or office in the church, that of _____.

269. (deacon) We have seen that in the local church there was a plurality of deacons. Commentaries say that the ministry of the presbyter is spiritual and that of the deacon is material. This distinction can be taken from Acts 6:2,4 in the following words, ". . . It is not desirable that we should leave the Word of God, and serve tables. . . but we will give ourselves continually to prayer and to the ministry of the word." Now let us consider the ministry of the _____.

270. (deacon) Let's read the passage in Acts 6:1-7. Did you read it? What a beautiful portion! What title in your Bible is given to this section? _____ chosen to _____.

271. (Seven, serve) Some consider these seven to be "deacons." Now the problem is that the word "deacon" does not appear in the text. Even though the word "deacon" does not appear in the section (and some,

because of this, say that it doesn't deal with the question of deacons) many believe the ministry they exercised was the work of _____.

272. (deacons) One thing is certain. The men chosen had a ministry, a responsibility, different than that of the apostles. This ministry was to "serve tables" (a diakonia) and included the daily distribution. These words, it seems, deal more with _____ things.

273. (material) This thought agrees with the qualifications of the bishops and the deacons in I Tim. 3. There it says that the bishop should be "apt to teach" but does not have this qualification for the deacon. The seven men in Acts 6 were chosen in order to "_____ tables."

274. (serve) Yes. They were chosen in order to free the apostles from secular work, or "serving tables." Certainly this does not mean to say that the deacons should not be spiritual men. Read again the words of Acts 6:3, ". . . seek out from among you seven men of good reputation, full of the Holy Spirit and wisdom . . . ." What are the necessary qualifications?

   1. _____ _____
   2. _____ of the _____ _____
   3. _____

275. (1. good reputation; 2. full, Holy Spirit; 3. wisdom) Very good! The deacons have to be spiritual men in order to exercise a "_____" ministry.

276. (serving) There are many other important considerations such as: the qualifications of bishops and deacons (I Tim. 3:1-13; Titus 1:5-9); the details and examples of their work; the choosing of elders and deacons. But our study is limited to this brief consideration. Our study in this lesson is about the _____ of the church.

277. (officials) The two officials (offices or positions) are the _____ and the _____.

278. (presbyters or elders, deacons) The other four names used for the Presbyter are: _____, _____, _____, _____.

279. (elder, bishop, overseer, pastor) Always there is a _____ of presbyters in the local church. (See items 264 and 265.)

280. (plurality) These men were chosen by the _____ _____.

281. (Holy Spirit) It seems that the service of the deacon is a _____

ministry of spiritual men.

282. (material)

Suggestions and Plan for the Group Study:

Lesson 10: The Officials of the Local Congregation: Elders (Presbyters, bishops, overseers, pastors) and Deacons

Plan:

1. Be sure the students have already studied the lesson or reserve time for study.

2. Read passages related to subject.

3. Use the following questions or references to motivate the exchange of ideas.

Questions and References:

1. What is the significance of the four names given for the presbyter?

2. What is the importance of the plurality of deacons and presbyters?

3. What are the qualifications of the presbyters (elders) and deacons according to I Tim. 3:1-13 and Titus 1:5-9?

4. What do you think? Were Timothy and Titus pastors of local churches or missionaries (evangelists or church planters)--colleagues of the Apostle Paul?

LESSON 11 DISCIPLINE OR SEPARATION
IN THE LOCAL CHURCH

Upon finishing this lesson, the student will be able to:

--Explain the teaching of Jesus in Matthew 18:15-20.

--State the reason for the church to separate itself from the erring brother.

--Understand better his responsibility in helping the erring brother.

283. In order to maintain health in the human body, it is necessary to feed the body and to be careful of illnesses that come in order to disrupt health. Also in the Body of Christ, the local church, needs to maintain spiritual health, be alert to the dangers that there are. In I Pet. 2:5, we read, "also, as living stones, are built up a spiritual house, a holy priesthood . . . ." This house is a _____ house.

284. (spiritual) Yes. It is a spiritual house. It is also a _____ priesthood.

285. (holy) In order to maintain a spiritual house and holiness, the local church must be careful of sin in the members. That which destroys the testimony of the local church is _____.

286. (sin) Yes. The sickness that disrupts vital church life is sin. Sometimes there are believers, members of the congregation, that persist in their sins. What should the congregation do? The topic of this lesson is _____ or _____ in the local church.

287. (discipline, separation) Let us return to the teaching of Jesus in Matthew 18:15-20. The title of this paragraph is, "_____ with a _____ _____."

288. (Dealing, Sinning Brother) We have already studied this passage from several view points. But now let's study the topic of the paragraph: "_____ ____ a _____ _____."

289. (Dealing with, Sinning Brother) Yes. It deals with the question of _____ or _____ from a brother in sin.

290. (discipline, separation) Ordinarily, we speak of the right of the local church to discipline its members and, possibly, this is right depending on the definitions we use. Correct definitions are: to correct character defects, to maintain order, to apply discipline to would be acceptable, but not in the sense of throwing out, excommunicating from the Body, or chastening (see Hebrews 12:5-11). Let us use "discipline" in the sense of

"separation" because only God has the right of _____ His children.

291. (chastening) Yes. God in His love disciplines us. Now let us consider the case in Matt. 18:15, "Moreover if your brother sins against you, go and tell him his fault between you and him alone. If he hears you, you have gained your brother." First, a note: The words "against you" are not in some manuscripts. Therefore, the reading may be, "and your brother sins" (See NASB). Now we note immediately the responsibility of every individual believer! If a brother or sister in the congregation, a member of the body of Christ, is living in sin (sins) and a believer knows this, it is his/her responsibility to go with love and humility and speak with the erring believer. When there is sin in the congregation every _____ _____ has a responsibility.

292. (individual believer) Yes. The believer has a responsibility; "go and reprove him (correct him), in private." We note also that this principle is a matter between two persons privately. It is not speaking of an erring brother behind his back but speaking with the person "face to face." It is speaking with the person _____.

293. (personally) In order to exercise this ministry, there must exist in the life

of the believer love, courage and obedience. We hope for a positive result: "If he hears you, you have gained your brother." If the person in sin repents and leaves his/her sin, it is good--the matter is finished! Thanks be to God! There is victory! The two brothers are again one in Christ. If the erring brother repents, the Word says, "you _____ _____ your _____."

294. (have gained, brother) What joy! There is one more problem resolved! The desire of every spiritual believer is a positive result. Sadly our human nature is very rebellious and self-centered. For this reason, it is difficult to be courageous in confronting others. Verse 16 states, "But if he will not hear you." What does the believer do if he is not able to gain his brother? The erring brother persists in his sin! What to do when the result is not positive but _____!

295. (negative) Reading on in the verse, ". . . take with you one or two more, that by the mouth of two or three witnesses every word may be established." This concept is from the Old Testament. (See Deut. 19:15.) If the believer does not have success in his desire of helping the brother in sin, he should take _____ or _____ _____ with him in order to deal with the matter.

296. (one, two witnesses) Did you get it right? Yes. The brother that knows of sin in the life of another has a _____.

297. (responsibility) If he/she does not succeed alone in dealing with the guilty person then he should take with him one or two spiritual persons in order to appeal again with the person. Without doubt two or three persons have more voice than just one! The word says, "that in the mouth of two or three witnesses, _____ _____ may be _____."

298. (every word, established) Now if the guilty one repents (confessing to God and the person against whom he has sinned) the problem is resolved. But if he/she still does not repent? Read verse 17, "and if he refuses to hear them, tell it to the church." If the guilty person still does not wish to hear, two or three should take the question before the _____.

299. (church) What a pity! It is sad! But when a believer does not wish to leave his sin, the church (the members in fellowship) must act. They call the person "to account." They call the person to a meeting of the members (the prayer meeting!). Again, if the believer makes right his/her life, great! The _____ is finished.

300. (matter) We note in all of this the love and patience of God. These

words are the teachings of _____.

301. (Jesus) But what happens if this believer in sin does not listen to the church? The last part of verse 17 says, "But if he refuses even to hear the church, let him be to you like heathen and a tax collector," or as an _____.

302. (unbeliever) The church has to separate itself from the person as though he/she were an unbeliever. This is separation of communion (fellowship) in the church. (It does not say from the meetings of the church!) They must deal with him/her as a _____ and _____ _____.

303. (heathen, tax collector) And how were the heathen (Gentiles) and tax collectors (publicans) dealt with by the Jews? They were positively treated badly! But how should believers deal with unbelievers? With the love of God in order to win them to Christ, without accepting sin. Briefly, we have studied the important teaching of the Lord Jesus about how we should _____ with a _____ _____."

304. (deal, sinning brother) This passage is very important and teaches us the steps that need to be taken in order to deal with a believer who offends another. We finish this passage with the words of Alexander R. Hay,

". . . The Lord is speaking of a case in which he who has sinned does not repent and doesn't wish to deal with the evil which he has committed. If he had done so, the matter would be finished. But as he does not wish to repent and as the matter cannot be left in this condition because sin in the congregation affects its communion with the Lord who is in the midst . . . " Matt. 18:15-20 is the teaching of the Lord _____.

305. (Jesus) Now let us consider other important passages concerning discipline or separation. Read I Cor. 5:1-13. Did you read it? Here there is a case of immorality. There is much teaching in this passage! Let us at least consider the basic principles and leave a full exegesis. In this passage there is a flagrant case of _____.

306. (immorality) Yes. It is the case of a brother in the church living in immorality and the church is doing nothing! Paul writes, ". . . there is sexual immorality among you . . . and you are puffed up and have not rather mourned, that he who has done this deed might be taken away from among you." The church should act! These are strong words, ". . . that he . . . might be _____ away from among you." (vs. 7, "purge out")

307. (taken) But, who has the responsibility? Verse 4 says, "In the name of

our Lord Jesus Christ, when you are gathered together . . . ." The one who has the responsibility is the _____.

308. (church) Yes. The congregation has the responsibility. This is a known case known by all and the brother does not wish to repent and leave his sin. (See Prov. 28:13.) He who has the responsibility to act is the _____ itself.

309. (church or congregation) And what should the congregation and the individual believers do? Verse 11, ". . . not to keep company with anyone named a brother, who is a fornicator . . . not even to eat with such a person." The congregation and the individual believer should _____ from the brother in sin.

310. (separate) It is the same responsibility of the congregation and the individual believer to separate from the person living in sin. Let us see another case. Read II. Thes. 3:6-15. In verses 6, 7 and 11 the word _____ is repeated.

311. (disorderly) Yes. Here we have the case of a brother walking disorderly. Without doubt the word "disorderly" has many applications. The problem in this section is the brother who is walking _____.

312. (disorderly) In the context what is the disorder? Verse 11 says, "For we hear that there are some who walk among you in a disorderly manner not working at all, but are busybodies." These are persons that do not wish to _____.

313. (work) They are lazy and "busybodies." What should the church do? Verse 6 says, ". . . withdraw from every brother who walks disorderly . . . ." And verse 14, ". . . and do not keep company with him . . . ." The congregation has to _____ _____.

314. (separate itself) And why the separation or discipline? ". . . that he may be ashamed." Remember that the purpose of separation is in order that the person might _____ and return to communion with Christ.

315. (repent) Verse 15 is a good warning and exhortation, "Yet do not count him as an enemy, but admonish him as a brother." This is good! Let us consider only one thing more. In Titus 3:10,11, we read, "Reject a divisive man after the first and second admonition, knowing that such a person is warped and sinning, being self-condemned." The case is of the believer who persists in dividing believers (it may be through teaching false doctrine). Paul says in verse 10, "_____ a divisive man."

316. (reject) Yes. In the case of a divisive person or false doctrine there should be an attempt to correct the error (admonition), but if there is no change the believer must _____ _____.

317. (separate himself) To finish this lesson let us at least cite two verses related with the study: Romans 15:1, "We then who are strong ought to bear with the scruples (weaknesses) of the weak, and not to please ourselves." And Gal. 6:1, "Brethren, if a man is overtaken in any trespass, you who are spiritual, restore such a one in a spirit of gentleness, considering yourself lest you also be tempted." The ones that have the greatest responsibility are the _____ and _____.

318. (strong, spiritual) The Lord Jesus teaches us in Matt. 18:15-20 the question of "Dealing with a _____ _____."

319. (Sinning Brother) After completing all the provisions or steps in helping the brother to repent of sin, if he doesn't repent, the church has to _____ from him.

320. (separate)

Suggestions and Plan for the Group Study:

Lesson 11: Discipline or Separation in the Local Church

Plan:

1. Be sure the students have already studied the lesson or reserve time for the study.

2. Read passages related to the subject.

3. Use the following questions or references to motivate the exchange of ideas.

Questions and References:

1. How should the brother in sin be dealt with if he doesn't wish to repent?

2. The students could discuss one by one the cases for discipline mentioned in the lesson.

3. The student should read carefully all the passage of I Cor. 5:1-13 and note the seriousness of these sins mentioned and the strong attitude of the Apostle Paul: vs. 5, ". . . deliver such a one to Satan" and vs. 13, "put

away."

4. In these days is discipline practiced as it should be practiced?

5. There is always the danger of disciplining for unbiblical reasons. We must be sure the sin is biblically explicit. Institutions, mission boards and churches may establish any "rules" or "traditions" they may as long as they do not claim them to be "biblical" (when they are not) and, therefore, motive for "church discipline".

LESSON 12   THE PRINCIPAL MISSION OF THE NEW TESTAMENT CHURCH AND ITS OWN GROWTH

Upon finishing this lesson, the student will be able to:

--- State the principal mission of the church.

--- Explain what the Great Commission is.

--- List the words that are expressions of the Great Commission.

--- Note the phrases that express the will of God in his life.

321. Good. We have studied various aspects of the Church, the Body of Christ, especially in its local aspect. We have considered something of its vital life internally, that which is necessary for its growth and maturity. What is the purpose and the function of this church, this Body, in the world? Our consideration will be the _____ of the church.

322. (mission) In order to better understand the mission of the church, let us use the Great Commission as an expression of God's will for the church. The mission of the church is expressed in the _____ _____.

323. (Great Commission) The Great Commission are the words of _____ _____.

324. (Jesus Christ) The main passages of Scripture are: Genesis 12:1-3 (see the reference at the end of the lesson); Matt. 28:18-20; Mark 16:15-16; Luke 24:47; John 20:21 and Acts 1:8. These passages speak to us of the _____ _____.

325. (Great Commission) Let us note that in Mark we have the words, "Go . . . and preach . . .;" in Luke , "should be preached . . .;" in John, ". . . I also send you;" and in Acts, ". . . and you shall be my witness . . . ." These words express the _____ _____.

326. (Great Commission) Let us use Matt. 28:19-20 as a base for our study: "<u>Go</u> ye therefore and <u>make disciples</u> of all the nations, <u>baptizing them</u> in the name of the Father, and of the Son, and of the Holy Spirit, <u>teaching them</u> to observe all things, that I have commanded you . . . ." (For our study now, we are not going to consider the authority of Jesus in Verse 18 nor the final promise in Vs . 20). The words underlined are: _____,_____ _____,_____ _____, _____ _____.

327. (Go make, disciples, baptizing them, teaching them) The words are words of _____ _____.

103

328. (Jesus Christ) Yes. The expressions of the mission of the church are: you shall be my witness, go, preach, make disciples, baptize them, teach them. They are the expressions of the _____ _____.

329. (Great Commission) Now here in Matthew, there are four verbs that show action; Go, make disciples, baptizing, and teaching. In our Bible the first two are in the imperative tense which expresses commands, (see number 2 of the questions) and the other two are participles (the general form) that expresses continuing action. In these verses, three methods of completing the will of God in the Great Commission are: go, baptize, teach. These activities are _____ of completing the goal.

330. (methods) Now what is the goal or end or purpose? "To make disciples" (or matheteusate--"disciple"). The goal or mission of the Great Commission is to _____ _____.

331. (make disciples) Yes. The mission of the church in the world is to go, preach the gospel, make disciples, baptize them, and teach them. The object is always to make more _____.

332. (disciples) The evangelistic goal of the church is to _____ _____, followers of Christ.

333. (make disciples) A disciple is a believer, or Christian, born again by the Holy Spirit, a true child of God. (I John 1:12-13; 3:5-7; Acts 11:26; Rom. 10:9). The will of God is that we (as the church of Christ) _____ _____.

334. (make disciples) The will of God is the growth of the true church (in quantity and quality). Yes. God's will is the _____ of the church.

335. (growth) The goal or main purpose of the church is to go and _____ _____.

336. (make disciples) In these verses there is a kind of circular motion which goes like this: "going (preach), make disciples, baptizing them, teaching them, to observe all things in order that they might go, (preach), make disciples, baptize, teach in order that they might . . . ." The mission of the church can be considered to be a _____ _____. (II Tim. 2:2)

337. (circular motion) Now our problem many times is that we stop the movement (the wheel) with necessary and important activities and we lose the vision of God's will in the Great Commission of making _____.

338. (disciples) The main purpose of the church is expressed in the _____ _____.

339. (Great Commission) Yes. We should preach to all the world that Christ saves the sinner. In order to finish our study, let us remember that God has a glorious purpose in the life of the individual believer while he is obeying His word and taking part in the activities of His church. Let us look at four expressions from the letters of the Apostle Paul:

". . . to be conformed to the <u>image of His Son</u> . . ." (Rom. 8:29).

". . . We are being transformed into the <u>same image</u> from glory to glory . . ." (II Cor. 3:18).

". . . Christ in you, the hope of glory." (Col. 1:27)

". . . that we may present every man perfect in Christ Jesus." (Col. 1:28)

God's will in your life is the _____ of His _____, that you might be _____ in _____.

340. (image, Son, perfect, Christ) May this study be a means of completing these purposes in your life! CONGRATULATIONS!

Suggestions and Plan for the Group Study:

Lesson 12: The principal mission of the New Testament Church

Plan:

1. Be sure the students have already studied the lesson or reserve time for the study.

2. Read passages related to the subject.

3. Use the following questions or references to motivate the exchange of ideas.

Questions and References:

1. In examining the Scriptures anew, one can observe God's desire to reach "all the families of the earth." Many believe that the "Great Commission" really begins with the Call of Abraham in Genesis 12:1-3.

    "Now the Lord had said to Abram: '. . . I will bless you . . . be a blessing . . . And in you all the families of the earth shall be blessed.'"

Discuss these concepts.

2. What is the Great Commission?

3. What are the main passages that express the mission of the church?

4. Study in a Bible Dictionary the word "disciple."

5. Discuss Matt. 28:19, ". . . disciples of all nations" (ethne)--all ethnic groups.

6. Discuss the concept: "Our God is a missionary God" and "the Bible is a missionary book."

7. What is God's will for your life?

APPENDICES:

1. Exams for the Study:

    Exam 1, Lessons 1-6

    Exam 2, Lessons 7-9

    Exam 3, Lessons 10-12

    Answers to Exams

2. The Synagogue:

    Form for the mission of the people of God among the nations.

3. Bibliography

The New Testament Church

Exam #1   **Lessons 1-6**

1. The church belongs to _____ _____.

2. A simpler definition of the local church is: "_____ or _____ gathered in _____ _____."

3. The local church is a part of the _____ _____.

4. The church began on the _____ of _____.

5. In the first local church in Jerusalem, the persons that received the _____ were _____.

6. Baptism is for those that _____ in Christ and the mode of baptism is by _____.

7. What are the four activities of the first local church?

    1) The _____ of the _____.

    2) _____.

    3) _____ of _____.

    4) _____.

8. In order to show fellowship in a practical way, the believer should be present in the _____ of the _____.

9. In the Lord's Supper, Jesus is _____.

10. At the Lord's Supper, we proclaim the _____ of _____ until He _____.

The New Testament Church

Exam #2   Lessons 7-9

1. Before partaking of the Lord's Supper, the believer has the responsibility of _____ and _____ himself.

2. In the first church they celebrated the Lord's Supper "_____ _____ _____."

3. For this reason, in the New Testament Church, the Lord's Supper should be celebrated at least each _____.

4. In the prayer meeting there is the promise of the _____ of Jesus.

5. The words "in accord" signify that the local church should have _____ in prayer.

6. In order to obtain answers to prayer, there are certain _____.

7. Which members of the church are priests? _____

8. We, who are believers, are the _____ of Christ and individually _____ of the same.

9. God gave gifts or manifestations of the Holy Spirit for
   _____
   _____.

10. What are the basic ministries of the New Testament Church?

   1) _____
   2) _____
   3) _____
   4) _____
   5) _____

The New Testament Church

Exam #3   Lessons 10-12

1. The two official places or positions in the church are _____ and _____.

2. In the New Testament, the four names that signify the same office are: 1)_____, 2)_____, 3)_____, 4)_____.

3. There is always a _____ of elders and deacons.

4. These men were chosen by the _____ _____.

5. In the local church, the word "discipline" means only _____ because only God has the right to punish His children.

6. The purpose of separation is to help the brother _____ and return to fellowship.

7. When a believer knows of a brother living in sin, he should: (Number the right order, leaving blank the wrong answers.)

   _____ Tell all to your wife or husband about the person.

   _____ Take the case to the church to resolve it in the prayer meeting.

   _____ Speak to the person in private.

_____ Recommend to the pastor that he should expose the person publicly.

_____ Take one or two witnesses in order to win the person.

_____ Say nothing to anyone.

8. The Great Commission defines the _____ of the church.

9. The purpose of the Great Commission is to _____ _____.

10. The four verbs used for completing the will of God, expressed in the Great Commission, are:

1) _____.
2) _____.
3) _____.
4) _____.

The New Testament Church

Exam #1   Answers to Exams

1. Jesus Christ
2. one, two, My, name
3. Universal Church
4. Day, Pentecost
5. Word, baptized
6. believe, immersion
7. 1) doctrine or teaching, apostles

    2) communion or fellowship

    3) breaking, bread

    4) prayers
8. activities or meetings, church
9. present
10. death, Christ, comes

Exam #2

1. examining, judging
2. every Lord's day
3. week or Sunday
4. presence
5. unanimity
6. conditions
7. all

8. Body, members

9. --the functioning of the church

    --the edification of the church

    --the good of the church

    --its growth, etc.

10. 1) apostles

    2) prophets

    3) evangelists

    4) pastors

    5) teachers

Exam #3

1. presbyters (elders), deacons

2. 1) Presbyter

    2) Elder

    3) Bishop or overseer

    4) Pastor

3. plurality

4. Holy Spirit

5. separation

6. repent

7. blank

    3

    1

blank

2

blank

8. purpose or goal

9. make disciples

10. 1) go, going

   2) make disciples or discipling

   3) baptizing

   4) teaching

THE SYNAGOGUE: FORM FOR THE MISSION
OF THE PEOPLE OF GOD AMONG THE NATIONS

by Sam Westman Burton

OUTLINE

Introduction

    I.   The Synagogue in Israel and Judaism

        A.   The Origin of the Synagogue
               The Exilic Period
               The Pre-exilic Period
               The Post-exilic Period

        B.   The Necessity and Purpose of the Synagogue

        C.   The Synagogue and the Israelite Mission to the Nations

    II.   The Synagogue and the New Covenant

        A.   Jesus Christ and His Use of the Synagogue

        B.   Paul's Use of the Synagogue for the Expansion of the Church among the Nations

    III.   The Synagogue Form as a Model for the New Testament Church: Vehicle for the Extension of the Redemptive Mandate Today

        A.   Testimony to History

        B.   The Synagogue Form and Cultural Anthropology Today

C. The Synagogue and House Churches: Conclusion

THE SYNAGOGUE: FORM FOR THE PEOPLE OF GOD AMONG THE NATIONS

Introduction

Writing of the synagogue, the Christian scholar, R.T. Herford, said, "No human institution has a longer unbroken history, and nothing has done more for uplifting the human race" (Hertz XVII). This outstanding statement shows the importance of the synagogue in human history. Another expression of this importance comes from Jewish tradition as quoted by Joseph Gutman, "as a gazelle leaps from place to place, and from fence to fence, and from tree to tree, and from booth to booth, so God jumps and leaps from synagogue to synagogue so that He may bless Israel" (IX). These two statements emphasize the fact that the God of history used the synagogue as His instrument for blessing and the mission of the people of God among the nations. This paper will trace its origins under the Old Covenant, its place in Judaism and spread throughout the nations under the New Covenant.

I. The Synagogue in Israel and Judaism

It is appropriate at the outset to define the word "synagogue." It comes from the Greek and means "assembly." However, when we go to Hebrew there is some confusion as to its meaning and identification. Eisenberg clears up much discussion and debate by combining three Hebrew expressions and identifying them with the synagogue. He writes, "there are three names for synagogue in Hebrew: Bet Tefilah, a House of Prayer; Bet Hamidrash, a

House of Study; and *Bet Haknesset*, a House of Assembly" (62). This is very helpful in considering the purpose and use of the synagogue in the nation of Israel.

A. The Origin of the Synagogue

When we come to the origin of the synagogue there is much scholarly work that has been done. Both Jewish and Christian scholars have taken one of three positions as to when the synagogue originated: exilic—during the Babylonian captivity in the sixth century B.C.; pre-exilic; or the post-exilic period (Gutman: 72). Without getting into too much detail, it might be helpful to consider thoughts from various scholars.

The Exilic Period

Kohler writes:

> The greatest and, indeed the unique creation of Judaism is the Synagogue . . . Devised in the Exile as a substitute for the Temple, it soon eclipsed as a religious force and a rallying point for the whole people (447).

We see here that Kohler not only holds the exilic position but with zeal gives us insight as to the missionary expansion of the synagogue.

Gutman writes:

> The argument for a Babylonian origin is based on the assumption that the loss of the Temple with its sacrificial cult offerings in 586 B.C. left a religious void that had to be filled while the Jews were in exile in Babylonia" (72).

Eisenberg writes:

It was Ezekiel who suggested the answer: 'True, I have not banished them far away and scattered them in the countries where they have settled' (Ezekiel 11:15-16). The prophet here assures us the exiles that they are not to be deprived of what is theirs, and that God is with them even in a land far from their own. But this statement also contains what may be a clue to the origin of the synagogue. The Hebrew word *Mikdash meaht*, translated 'little sanctuary,' is believed by the rabbis to refer to the synagogue. (30-31)

The Pre-exilic Period

Regarding the pre-exilic position, there are those who believe that there is expression of the need of such an institution before the Exile. Some would even trace the origin back to Moses. James spoke at the Jerusalem Council, "For from early generations Moses has had in every city those who preach him, for he is read every Sabbath in the synagogues." (Acts 15:21) "Josephus, Philo and later Judaism traced the synagogue back to Moses" (Tenny: 817).

Another thought is expressed by De Ridder, "The origin must be found in the need for secular and spiritual assemblies even in pre-exilic times." (78). He also mentions that meeting together was not a new thing among the Jews. There is the case of the Shunnamite asking her husband, "Why will you go to him (Elisha) today?" (II Kings 4:23). The priests and levites also went on circuits to instruct the people (II Chronicles 17:9).

The Post-exilic Period

The post-exilic position is argued from the fact of the existence of the synagogue throughout Diaspora (Dispersion) and the Intertestamental period. Perhaps it is during this time of judgement and sadness for Israel that the psalmist writes, "they said in their hearts, let us destroy them together; they have burned up all the synagogues of God in the land" (Psalm 74:8).

In conclusion, we must agree with Gutman, "The synagogue, whose time and place of origin are shrouded in mystery" (72) and De Ridder, "the origin of the Synagogue is acknowledged to be lost in obscurity" (78). However, though it cannot be established for certain the time of the origin of the synagogue, its existence and importance is indisputable.

B. The Necessity and Purpose of the Synagogue: Survival, School, Worship, Discipline

The synagogues of the Diaspora were necessary for the survival of Judaism. They were necessitated by the need of communal worship and instruction after the destruction of the Temple (Zeitlin in Gutman: 73).

> Scattered and dispersed among the nations, the Jews could maintain their existence and national features only as long as the organization of their internal life was of sufficient strength to serve as a barrier against the

> influences of the alien environment (De Ridder: 76).

> Both Philo and Josephus say that the purpose of the Synagogue was to promote the moral and religious education of the community . . . in ordinary speech the school and Synagogue were so closely associated that the two were not distinguished (81).

"The synagogue has always been the center of Jewish life communally, religiously and educationally" (Eisenberg: 62).

The synagogue did not mean only survival in the Disaspora and schools for instruction but also the true worship of Yahweh. "In the meetings in the synagogue there seems to have been a great deal of freedom as to who should make the address" (Norbie: 19).

> During the Exile and afterward the people assemble on the Sabbath to hear the word of God read from the Torah and the prophets and to join in prayer and song, which soon became a permanent institution (Kohler: 457).

Not only was the institution of the synagogue the center of education and worship, it also became the center of "community" and "local" discipline (cf. Matthew 10:17; 23:34; Mark 13:9; Luke 21:12). The Diaspora Colonies were given some authority to govern and determine their own affairs. "The synagogue community appears to have been the center of this discipline, especially when it concerned religious matters of Jewish law" (De Ridder: 96).

C. The Synagogue and the Israelite Mission to the Nations

God spoke to Abraham, "I will bless thee . . . and thou shalt be a blessing . . . and in thee shall all families of the earth be blessed" (Genesis 12:2-3). How did the synagogue fit into the fulfillment of this commission and command? Was the synagogue a blessing among the nations? De Ridder suggests: "It (the synagogue) was developed for the needs of the believing community but was undoubtedly often consciously adapted to the needs of the foreigner" (78).

The foreigner!!

> The origins of Jewish proselytism must be found in the regulations for

> the treatment of the stranger in the Promised Land . . . the word ger (a resident alien) came to mean proselyte . . . The Diaspora . . . presented a unique opportunity for the nations to attach themselves in varying relationships to the Jewish faith and people (88).

Yes, undoubtedly the synagogue was a blessing among the nations. Though Judaism was more a survival movement than a missionary movement, yet there was, in some respects, a "leavening" effect. "Proselytes were accepted as full members of the community" (90).

The Septuagint (LXX) made it possible for the Greek world to read the Old testament in the Greek vernacular. The Synagogue started Judaism on its world-mission and made the Torah the common property of the entire people (Kohler: 447). "The Synagogue was limited to no one locality, like the Temple, but raised its banner wherever the Jews settled throughout the globe" (448).

Though the synagogue helped spread the monotheism of the Jews and the ethical teachings of the Mosaic Law to all nations, by the time of our Lord it was not but a mixed blessing. Jesus spoke harsh words to the scribes and Pharisees of His day.

> Woe unto you, scribes and Pharisees, hypocrites! For ye compass sea and land to make one proselyte, and when he is made, ye make him twofold more the child of hell than yourselves" (Matthew 23:15).

Though there may well have been groups of scribes and Pharisees who traveled for proselytizing, Judaism was not a "Missionary movement." As De Ridder writes, "We may not conclude . . . that Judaism was a missionary religion in the modern sense." (95). Yes, Israel failed in being the blessing they should have been to the nations. Yes, Judaism through the synagogue failed. But, God in sovereignty and grace ordained that "through their fall salvation is come unto the gentiles" (Romans 11:11).

II.   The Synagogue and the New Covenant

By the time of the appearance of the Messiah, Son of David, Son of Man, Suffering Servant, the synagogue was an established institution throughout the Roman World. Zeitlin explains well the debt that Christianity has toward the Judaism of the first century: "Christianity with its institutions is directly traceable to the Judaism of that period. The Church, the institution of Christianity, is a daughter of the synagogue" (Gutman: 69).

This paper will trace some of the uses of the synagogue in the life of Jesus Christ and the Apostle Paul and its significance for the Church today. As a beginning summary statement of the effectiveness of the synagogue and its place in the first century world Tenny writes the following:

> How effectively the synagogue, along with the school, fulfilled this purpose is to be seen 1) from the survival of Judaism, 2) from the thorough judaistic nature of Galilee in the first century which in the time of Simon Maccabeus was largely pagan, and 3) from the knowledge of the scriptures which the Apostle Paul assumes of his hearers in the Hellenistic synagogues (818).

A. Jesus Christ and His Use of the Synagogue

> The Scriptures are the main historical source for consideration of Jesus' relationships with the synagogue. It is not the place here to observe how Jesus was born into Judaism, baptized by John "to fulfill all righteousness" and consider His relationship to the Temple and temple worship.
>
> In the Gospels Jesus is found attending the synagogue in various places and initiating His ministry from the "freedom of the synagogue." Some examples are the following:

All Galilee

"And Jesus went about all Galilee teaching in their synagogues, and preaching in the gospel of the kingdom, and healing all manner of sickness" (Matthew 4:23; 9:35; Luke 4:15,44).

Capernaum

"And they went into Capernaum, and straightway on the Sabbath day he entered into the synagogue and taught" (Mark 1:21; Luke 4:33; John 6:59).

Nazareth

"And he came to Nazareth, where he had been brought up; and as his custom was, he went into the synagogue on the Sabbath day, and stood up for to read" (Luke 4:16; Matthew 13:45; Mark 6:2). In these passages there is the significant phrase, "As his custom was" and also his being questioned as to his person "is not this the carpenter."

Jerusalem (apparently)

"And he entered again into the synagogue, and there was a man there which had a withered hand" (Mark 3:1; Matthew 12:9).

From the synagogue "platform" Jesus taught his disciples and the people. He delivered great discourses concerning Himself (Luke 4:16-18), and attitudes toward "positions" in the synagogue (Matthew 23:6; Luke 11:43; 20:46). Jesus said to the high priest, "I spake openly to the world; I even taught in the synagogue, and in the temple, whither the Jews always resort" (John 18:20). As Jesus used the temple and the synagogue as places for teaching and ministry and the extending of the Kingdom so the Apostles began their ministry from Temple and synagogue preaching. Speaking of the significance of Pentecost, Boer writes:

> At Pentecost they (the Jews gathered from many nations) began to be resolved into the "people of God" as the message of the gospel was addressed to the Jewish representatives of the nations of the world . . . at Pentecost they began to enter into the fellowship of the new Israel (138).

And thus the 'people of God' became the Church of the living God, the Body of Christ.

And the missionary movement grew and expanded from "Jerusalem and all Judea and Samaria and unto the uttermost part of the earth" (Acts 1:8). Paul, the Apostle to the Gentiles, went everywhere preaching the word. But, how did Paul begin his ministry? Where did he begin his preaching and teaching?

B. Paul's Use of the Synagogue for the Expansion of the Church Among all Nations

> The presence of believing communities throughout the world brought together in loyalty to the Truth, the availability of the Scriptures in translation and interpretation in the synagogues, the relative simplicity of the synagogue service, the synagogue itself . . . these are but a few . . . benefits from which Christianity would profit when the time was fulfilled that God 'sent forth His Son, born of woman, born under law, to redeem' (Galatians 4:4) (De Ridder: 127).

This is why the Apostle Paul used the synagogue as a starting point for missionary expansion. The evidence in scripture (using the history in Acts) is abundant concerning his contact with the synagogue:

Damascus

"Saul . . . desired of him letters to Damascus to the Synagogues, that if he found any of this way, whether they were men or women" (9:2). This verse not only shows Paul's going to the synagogue in order to persecute but also that the believers were still attending the synagogue worship, etc. Then, after Paul's conversion, he immediately begins his ministry in the synagogue. "And straightway he preached Christ in the synagogues that He is the Son of God" (9:20). Some years later Paul and Barnabas are "sent forth by the Holy Spirit" for their evangelizing, missionary journeys.

Salamis

"And when they were at Salamis, they preached the word of God in the synagogues of the Jews" (13:5).

Antioch in Pisidia

"They came to Antioch in Pisidia, and went into the synagogue . . . and after the reading of the law and the prophets the rulers of the synagogue sent unto them saying ye men and brethren, if ye have any word of exhortation for the people, say on" (Acts 13:14-15).

And Paul gave his excellent message on justification by faith. "And when the Jews were gone out of the synagogue, the Gentiles besought that these words might be preached to them" (Acts 13:42). "Many of the Jews and religious proselytes followed Paul and Barnabas . . . but . . . (other) Jews . . . were filled with envy" (13:43,45).

From these beginnings in the synagogue Paul began his evangelizing ministry. He became what some would call a "synagogue splitter" and from the "split" the local congregations were established.

Iconium

"And it came to pass in Iconium that they went both together into the synagogue of the Jews, and so spake, that a great multitude both of the Jews and also of the Greeks believed" (14:1). From Iconium, because of persecution, the missionaries traveled on to Lystra and Derbe where they preached the Gospel "and when they had ordained them elders in every church and had prayed with fasting, they commended them to the Lord, on whom they believed" (14:23).

After the Council at Jerusalem (Acts 15), Paul and Silas (not Barnabas) start out on another excursion. Their travels carried them back to Lystra (where Timothy joined the missionary company) and Iconium, through the region of Galatia and Asia, until they came to Troas. After the "Macedonian Vision" the group (now joined by Luke—16:10), traveled on to Philippi where (apparently) there was no synagogue (Acts 16:13). With the establishing of a work in Philippi the missionaries move on to Thessalonica, "where was a synagogue of the Jews; and Paul, as his manner was, went in . . . and . . . reasoned with them out of the scriptures" (17:1-2). And there was response to the gospel message preached, "some of them believed . . . but the Jews which believed not" (17:4,5). And on they traveled.

Berea

"Paul and Silas went into the synagogue of the Jews" (17:10).

Athens

"Paul . . . therefore disputed in the synagogue of the Jews" (17:17).

Corinth

"After these things Paul departed from Athens, and came to Corinth . . . and he reasoned in the synagogue" (18:1,4).

Ephesus

"And he came to Ephesus . . . and entered into the synagogue, and reasoned with the Jews" (18:19). Later on, coming back to Ephesus from a trip to Jerusalem "he went into the synagogue, and spoke boldly for the space of three months, disputing and persuading the things concerning the Kingdom of God" (19:8).

The scriptures testify the importance of the synagogue in the onward movement of the Gospel among the peoples of the world. They testify of the transition from Judaism and the synagogue to the assembly, the congregation, the Church, the "called out ones" of the New Testament (the new covenant in the blood of Jesus Christ).

> With the advent of Christianity, which regarded Jesus as the Messiah, a parting of the ways began. Little by little the Jewish

> Christians were alienated from the congregation of Israel. Their exclusion was necessary to preserve the unity of the Jews and to prevent the Jewish faith from being swallowed up by Christianity" (Eisenberg: 50).

The truths considered in the study of the synagogue under the Old and New Covenants have application for the ongoing of the gospel in any culture!

III. The Synagogue Form as a Model for the New Testament Church: Vehicle for the Extension of the Redemptive Mandate Today

    A. Testimony to History

The early local church adopted the simple form of the synagogue as its own. "The close relationship between the Church and the synagogue is shown . . . by James . . . in writing to Christian Jews he refers to the local church as a synagogue (James 2:2)" (Norbie: 21). "The form of worship of the synagogue was adopted by both the Christian and Muslim religions, and that form in its general outline is to be found today in their places of worship" (Tenny: 819).

Alex R. Hay writes:

> It should be borne in mind that the structure of the local church was based upon that of

the synagogue. The changes introduced are only such as the new spiritual order made necessary. The College of Elders, the "ministers" (servants—termed Deacons in the Church) and the freedom for any to take part in the preaching and teaching, which were the essential features of the synagogue, were the essential features also of the local church. In the Christian congregation there was no Chief Ruler or President; that place was occupied by the Lord who was present in the midst (134).

The fundamental difference between the synagogue and the local church is that in the church, as a result of the work accomplished on the Cross, Christ is present in the midst and His Holy Spirit dwells in each member, manifesting Himself through each one by the gifts of the Spirit" (280).

B. The Synagogue Form and Cultural Anthropology Today

One of the strong arguments against biblical forms today comes from the science of cultural anthropology. It is argued that the New Testament is steeped in the culture of the day, Roman government and law, Greek language and culture and Jewish religious systems. Therefore, Jesus and the Apostles and the writers of the New Testament were subject to the cultural forms of their day. This, of course, is true.

The conclusion, therefore, is that the forms of worship in the New Testament are not applicable today. It is stated that the church must be "indigenous" and adopt cultural forms within the context of the expanding church.

> It has been concluded by some that no definite or permanent form of Church organization is given in the New Testament. It is suggested that, at the time of the apostles, church organization was still rudimentary in form and only in process of formation and that it was God's purpose that it should be developed and perfected later as the need arose. (Hay: 133)

C. The synagogue and House Churches: Conclusion

It is being suggested in this paper that God, in His Sovereignty and wisdom, chose the culture of New Testament times for a specific purpose; that when Paul writes, "But when the fullness of the time was come, God sent forth His Son, made of a woman, made under the law" (Galatians 4:4), that he was suggesting a specific time in culture. It is suggested that the synagogue form is simple enough to fit any "tribe" or nation of people, any group of people meeting together. It is true that in Judaism the synagogue later meant "buildings" also. Jesus spoke of the "Chief seats" and "uppermost seats" in the synagogue (Matthew 23:6; Luke 20:46). Speaking of synagogues built after the first century, Eisenberg writes:

> The synagogues of this period were built on high ground. They usually consisted of a two-story building surrounded by a courtyard, with an outer staircase leading to an upper gallery for the women (51).

What is being suggested here is not the physical building (and there's nothing wrong with a building as such) but the simple, and very adequate form of synagogue worship and study. Could not this be the "wave of the future" in every country and society? Actually, here in the United States, there is a startling return to the "house" church and this also has biblical precedence.

Floyd V. Filson has some interesting thoughts along this line. He writes:

> These studies are useful and necessary. However, all of them would be still more fruitful, and the New Testament church would be better understood, if more attention were paid to the actual physical conditions under which the first Christians met and lived . . . the importance and function of the house church should be carefully considered. The assembly of

Christians in hospitable homes goes back to the very first days of the church. References in Acts (1:13; 2:26; 5:42; etc.) to such gatherings are only what would be expected. (105-106) (cf. also the Epistles)

He is quite contemporary when he further writes, "For all ordinary occasions, at least, the total body would split into smaller groups which could be housed in private homes . . . only rarely could a public assembly hall be obtained (Acts 19:9)" (106).

Certainly, a return to simplicity could save on the huge building constructions of the "Super-Churches." Even the "Super-Churches" recognize the need for "small groups" or "clusters." In these groups could there not be the application of "synagogue form" and worship?

In Conclusion, the words of Kohler express the "heart" of the "true Israel" in synagogue community and worship:

> In the synagogue was fanned the holy flame which kindled the heart with love of God and fellow men; here were offered sacrifices more pleasing to God than the blood and fat of beasts, sacrifices of love and charity (448).

Amen! May it be so in the churches of Jesus Christ today.

Postscript: Theological Education by Extension (TEE) is a very viable possibility for training "lay leaders" in simple "house" church structures.

Bibliography for Synagogue

Journal and Magazine Articles

Americas, June-July 1979. 25-28.

God Who Acts, London SCM Press, 1952. 15-32.

International Review of Mission. Vol. LXIII No. 270, April 1979. 102-118.

The Calvin Theological Journal, No. 2, Vol. IV, 1969. 23-50.

The Gordon Review, No. 2, Vol. XI, 1957. 40-52.

The Journal of Biblical Literature, No. 2, Vol. LVIII, 1939. 105-112.

Books

Boer, Harry R. *Pentecost and Missions*. Grand Rapids: Wm. B. Eerdmans Publishing Co., 1975.

Bright, John. *The Kingdom of God*. Nashville: Abingdon, 1953.

De Ridder, Richard R. *Discipling the Nations*. Grand Rapids: Baker Book House, 1975.

Eisenberg, Aziel. *The Synagogue Through the Ages*. New York: Bloch Publishing Company, 1974.

Gutman, Joseph. *The Synagogue: Studies in Origins, Archaeology and Architecture*. New York: KTAV Publishing House, Inc., 1975.

Hay, Alex Rattray. *The New Testament Order for Church and Missionary*. Welland: New Testament Missionary Union, 1947.

Kohler, K. *Jewish Theology*. New York: MacMillan Company, 1918.

Ladd, George Eldon. *The Gospel of the Kingdom*. Grand Rapids: Wm. B. Eerdmans Publishing Company, 1977.

Norbie, Donald L. *The New Testament Church Organization*. Kansas City: Walterick Publishers.

Satan Revealed In His Kosmos Today. "Man and God's Eternal Purpose". 1978.

Tenny, Merrill C. *The Zondervan Pictorial Bible Dictionary*. Grand Rapids: Zondervan Publishing House, 1963.

Wright, G. Ernest. *The Old Testament Against Its Environment*. Bloomsbury Street: SCM Press Ltd.

Bibliography

Boer, Harry R., <u>Pentecost and Missions</u>, Grand Rapids, Wm. B. Eerdmans Publishing Co., 1975.

Broadbent, E. H., <u>The Pilgrim Church</u>, London, Pickering and Inglis, 1931.

Bruce, F. F., <u>Commentary on the Book of Acts</u>, Grand Rapids, Wm. B. Eerdmans Publishing Co., 1983.

Carmichael, Amy, <u>Gold Cord</u>, London, SPCK, 1955.

Darby, J. N., <u>Synopsis of the Books of the Bible</u>, Kingston--ON--Thames, Stow Hill Bible and Tract Depot, 1948.

De Ridder, Richard R., <u>Discipling the Nations</u>, Grand Rapids, Baker Book House, 1975.

Edersheim, <u>Life and Times of Jesus the Messiah</u>, London, Longmans, 1886.

Eisenberg, Aziel, <u>The Synagogue through the Ages</u>, New York, Block Publishing Company, 1974.

Fisher, <u>History of the Christian Church</u>, New York, Charles Scribner's Sons, 1887.

Hay, Alex. Rattray, <u>The New Testament Order for Church and Missionary</u>, Welland, New Testament Missionary Union, 1947.

<u>Holy Bible, The</u>, New King James Version, Nashville, Thomas Nelson Publishers, 1983.

Kaller, Donald W., <u>Analise da Renovacao Pentecostal</u>, Patrocinio, CEIBEL, 1976.

Kohler, Dr. K., <u>Jewish Theology</u>, New York, MacMillan Company, 1918.

Latourette, Kenneth Scott, <u>A History of Christianity</u>, New York, Harper and Row Publishers, 1953.

Martin, Jose, <u>A Igreja</u>, Patrocinio, CEIBEL, 1975.

McMillan, William M., <u>Doutrina da Igreja</u>, Brazil, Instituto Biblico Mineiro, 1975.

Morgan, Campbell, <u>The Acts of the Apostles</u>, London, Pickering and Inglis, 1930.

Norbie, Donald F., <u>Early Church, The</u>, Waynesboro, Christian Missions Press, 1983.

<u>Ryrie Study Bible, The</u>, New American Standard, Chicago, Moody Press, 1976.

Tenney, Merrill C., <u>The Zondervan Pictorial Bible Dictionary</u>, Grand Rapids, Zondervan Publishing House, 1963.

Winter, Ralph D. and Steven C. Hawthorne, <u>Perspectives on the World Christian Movement</u>, Pasadena, William Carey Library, 1981.